Handbook of Mobile Application Development: A Guide to Selecting the Right Engineering and Quality Features

Authored by

Mohamed Sarrab

Hafedh Al-Shihi

&

Naveen Safia

Communication and Information Research Center
Sultan Qaboos University
Oman

Handbook of Mobile Application Development:
A Guide to Selecting the Right Engineering and Quality Features

Authors: Mohamed Sarrab, Hafedh Al-Shihi and Naveen Safia

ISBN (Online): 978-981-4998-24-6

ISBN (Print): 978-981-4998-25-3

ISBN (Paperback): 978-981-4998-26-0

need for a court order if at any point you breach any terms of this License Agreement. In no event will any delay or failure by Bentham Science Publishers in enforcing your compliance with this License Agreement constitute a waiver of any of its rights.

3. You acknowledge that you have read this License Agreement, and agree to be bound by its terms and conditions. To the extent that any other terms and conditions presented on any website of Bentham Science Publishers conflict with, or are inconsistent with, the terms and conditions set out in this License Agreement, you acknowledge that the terms and conditions set out in this License Agreement shall prevail.

Bentham Science Publishers Pte. Ltd.
80 Robinson Road #02-00
Singapore 068898
Singapore
Email: subscriptions@benthamscience.net

BENTHAM SCIENCE

CONTENTS

FOREWORD

Mobile applications have become ubiquitous and are present in almost all of today's business domains and life aspects. With the increasing prevalence of handheld computing devices (*e.g.*, smartphones), the growth of mobile applications is expected to continue, which will have an impact on academia and industry expectations and standards. That means we, as communities, need more proficient developers to design and develop more efficient, reliable, and secure mobile applications and relevant technologies and platforms.

This book will be a great addition to the literature to serve as a practical reference for students, researchers, and business communities who have an interest in learning about mobile computing and its features and design aspects. The book is written in a concise and conversational style that is easy to read and understand even though it discusses a great deal of very difficult relevant concepts from technical and design perspectives. The book talks about introductory topics such as the potential and the features of mobile general-purpose systems as well as very advanced concepts, including performance and security of mobile applications and the roadblocks expected during their evolution process.

Another interesting area the authors cover in this book is the quality, practicality, and effectiveness metrics that should be considered when evaluating mobile software systems. The solid research experience professor Sarrab has on mobile development and software system research speaks volumes about the effectiveness, practicality, and quality of the research findings introduced in this book.

I believe that this will be a good contribution to academia, research, and industry communities. I believe readers who are interested in getting familiar with and exposed to the mobile application's development life cycle and challenges will like it and will use it as a valuable reference. In academia, the book can also be used as a textbook for a course on mobile computing literacy and quality. I anticipate that a broader audience from industry-oriented communities, people who want to educate themselves on the topic, and also users who plan to take advantage of mobile applications to run their business operations and expand their customer populations will find this book to be very interesting and useful.

In short, the book has a lot to offer to both communities from academia and industry and is a valuable addition to the literature. It is written in a very practical and concise manner that makes it easy to read and a great one to carry as a reference.

Saleh M. Alnaeli
University of Wisconsin-Stout
Menomonie, Wisconsin
USA

PREFACE

This handbook is a complete encyclopedia about engineering requirements and quality characteristics that users, developers, and marketers of mobile applications should be aware of, and it provides detailed definitions, descriptions, and those features that overlap and are often confused. Today almost everyone uses a mobile phone with a good number of applications. However, not everyone knows its full advantage. In addition, this book helps in exploiting all the apps efficiently, thereby optimizing their use. Sometimes, when one buys a latest phone from a simpler version, it is so confusing that it is common to make mistakes. Some of these mistakes are undone easily, but some have locked the device to be made accessible by the distributor, and still, some are locked forever. Especially if you have bought it in one place and traveled to another country/continent. Mobile apps are distinguished, and studies are divided into eight different angles: capability, reliability, usability, charisma, security, performance, mobility, and compatibility. They are further divided into subsections for clarity. Every chapter has an introduction to all points discussed and a picture projects the different subsections in a user-friendly way. It not only describes each function but also sheds light on the perceptions of users. It is completely from the user's perspective. It is extremely useful to developers as it does highlight some performance issues like delay issue if the user misuses the app, he blames the app for 2 to 3 seconds of waiting time which is considered as delay, while a computer start time is about a minute with much more performance capacity. Also, the challenges are different types of users, different mobile phones with different capacities, with much varied and continually updated mobile apps.

This guide shows you how to:

1. Think through the design instead of just throwing UI elements.
2. Allow an intuitive design flow to emerging from your app.
3. Sketch and wireframe apps more effectively.
4. Reflect key differences among smartphones, tablets, and desktops.
5. Design for visual appeal without compromising usability.
6. Work effectively with programmers.
7. Make sure your apps are accessible to everyone.
8. Get usable feedback, and understand what it is telling you.
9. Learn valuable lessons from today's most successful apps.
10. Refresh your designs in new apps and future versions.
11. Discover new tools for designing more successfully.

CONSENT FOR PUBLICATION

Not applicable.

CONFLICT OF INTEREST

The authors [*Mohamed Sarrab,Hafedh Al-Shihi,* and *Naveen Safia*] of the enclosed manuscript titled: "Handbook of Mobile Application Development: A Guide to Selecting the Right Engineering, and Quality Features" have research support from The Research Council - Sultanate of Oman. Project [code: ORG/ICT/13/002]. Project title: M-Learning in Oman: Development, Adoption, and Dissemination..

ACKNOWLEDGEMENTS

In the name of Allah, the Most Gracious and the Most Merciful, I give thanks to Him for supporting us with the strength to complete this book. Without His support, none of this effort would have been possible. This book could not have been possibly completed without the recommendations, support, and advice of many people.

The idea for this book was generated because of the mobile learning research project. This research project is funded by The Research Council (TRC) of the Sultanate of Oman: under Grant No: ORG/SQU/ICT/13/006, (www.trc.gov.om). Project details are attached in appendix I. Thanks to The Research Council (TRC) of the Sultanate of Oman for taking a leadership role in this innovative research and for funding this important mobile learning project.

Mohamed Sarrab

Hafedh Al-Shihi

&

Naveen Safia
Communication and Information Research Center
Sultan Qaboos University
Oman

DEDICATION

Dedicated to
This book is dedicated to,
All mobile application developers.

Especially the great ones.

CHAPTER 1

Capability: Can Mobile Application Perform Valuable Functions?

Abstract: This chapter discusses the capability of a mobile application as one of the main qualitative characteristics. The chapter focuses on the completeness of the mobile application and the availability of all important functions. The features of accuracy and the efficiency of performance in mobile applications are explored and discussed. This chapter focuses on the best way in which the different features interact with each other and discusses the ability to perform multiple parallel tasks at the same time. Besides, this chapter pays emphasis to the support provided to all possible data formats. Finally, it discusses the ability to add features or change the current behavior of the application.

Keywords: Accuracy, Application Behavior, Capability, Completeness, Efficiency, Mobile Application, Multiple Parallel Tasks, Performance, Qualitative Characteristics.

1. INTRODUCTION

This chapter focuses on the capability of a mobile application as one of the main qualitative characteristics. The chapter is divided into seven sections. Section 1.1 is the introduction and section 1.2 is a pictorial representation of all the subsections of the chapter. Section 1.3 discusses in detail the completeness of the mobile application and the availability of all important functions. Section 1.4 explores the feature of accuracy in the mobile application. Section 1.5 discusses the efficiency of performance in a mobile application. Section 1.6 mainly focuses on the best way in which the different features interact with each other. Section 1.7 discusses the ability to perform multiple parallel tasks at the same time and section 1.8 focuses on the support provided to all possible data formats. Finally, section 1.9 discusses the ability to add features or change the current behavior of the application.

Mohamed Sarrab, Hafedh Al-Shihi and Naveen Safia

2. CAPABILITY

Generally, the capability of a mobile application is to measure the ability of the final product of the application to achieve its objectives, especially concerning its overall mission, in which the product shows the ability to perform valuable functions. The capability of mobile applications can be measured through seven parameters. They are completeness, accuracy, efficiency, interoperability, concurrency, data agnosticism, and extensibility, as shown in Fig. (**1**).

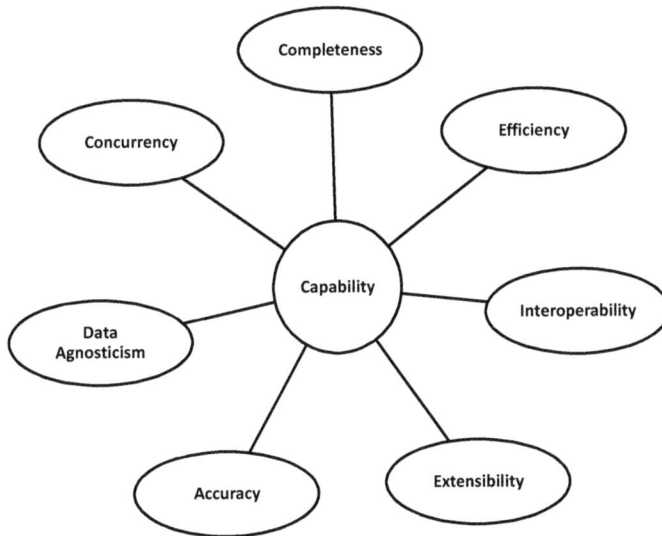

Fig. (1). Mobile Application Capability Factors.

Completeness refers to the availability of all functions the end-users want. On the other hand, accuracy is concerned with the correctness of the produced output in the right format. The efficiency of the mobile application is about the functions it performs efficiently, while interoperability considers the best way in which different features interact with each other. The feature of concurrency in the mobile application is concerned with the ability to perform multiple tasks at the same time and run parallel to other processes. Data agnosticism is about supporting different data formats, while extensibility is the ability to extend its features. The mobile application allows specific customers or third parties to change behavior or add additional features.

3. COMPLETENESS

The completeness of a mobile application is concerned with the availability of all important functions that are required by the stakeholders. It is a developed application component, where each function is described by a specification of the mobile application and which can be achieved by at least one functional execution path, operate as specified, and in as much detail as possible. Checking the mobile application for completeness is a very critical process as the specified application requirements have been developed and documented based on functions of all mobile applications, which are required to satisfy the stakeholder's objectives with their associated environmental performance, and other non-functional characteristics of the mobile application.

A specification is comprehensive, complete if all parts exist, and every part is completely developed. There are many properties that a mobile software specification must exhibit to ensure its completeness. To check the completeness of the mobile application, it is important to verify whether there are missing functions that are part of the developed application, but they are not called for in the specification's missing. Thus, the process of completeness of the mobile application varies if all the necessary components of the application are available and if any application process fails due to lack of resources or programming. The final product of the mobile application is a complete implementation of the functional specification. The functional specification is an official document for developers, which describes the intended capabilities of the targeted application in detail and the way of interaction with the users

The functional specification can be defined as a type of manual, guideline, or continuing reference point for the application developer. A tool for tracing requirements can be used to check the completeness of the mobile application if designers, engineers, and stakeholders feel the specified requirements meet the objectives. The requirement tracing is conducted throughout the development cycle of the application, which can be confirmed at each technical review for all old and new requirements.

The process of completeness verification checks the application's functional performance, environmental interface, operations and maintenance support, training, development, testing, production, deployment, as well as non-functional features such as availability, reliability, safety, and security. The purpose of tracing requirements is to ensure that the requirements continue to meet the needs and expectations of the stakeholders of the application (Margaret, 2007).

4. ACCURACY

Accuracy of a mobile application is concerned with the output of whether calculation in the product is correct and is presented with significant digits. It is about providing the right or agreed-on results or effects with the desired degree of precision. This can be measured by an attribute in the source code of the mobile application. Thus it is delegated to the components of the mobile application, which defines the functions that compute the values. Accuracy and precision are at times used interchangeably to describe the measurement errors. Essentially, precision is about the number of digits of a measurement that means something substantial. To build software for a mobile application, the developers are precise if they develop what has been agreed. However, they are accurate if what they build meets the client's business needs and solves a business problem.

Precision and accuracy are both essential in mobile applications. Perhaps the best technique to differentiate between the two concepts is that accuracy is the mapping of the application of business needs to the programmer model, while precision is the mapping of the programmer model of the problem back to the mobile model. However, though the two concepts are needed, accuracy is much harder to obtain. Practically, every development in mobile application either makes developments that are more accurate or more precise.

In practice, precision is significantly needed; however, accuracy is much more important. There are some techniques to improve accuracies such as issue tracking software, specification writing, spring and other dependency injection tools, and IDEs. A well-written specification of a mobile application allows both the application developers and users to understand the objectives of the application and the product. This helps to correct invalid notions by mobile application users at an early stage. However, in case a specification is too much in detail, it can be used as a precision justification at the cost of accuracy. The spring and dependency injection tools reduce the costs of changing code for accuracy in a mobile application.

Accuracy and precision are not necessarily directly proportional. For instance, high accuracy does not essentially indicate high precision nor does high precision imply high accuracy. But both high precision and high accuracy will make the product too expensive. Two additional terms need to be defined regarding precision and accuracy. They are data quality and errors. Data quality is concerned with the precision and accuracy of user data and error encompasses both the imprecision of data and its inaccuracies. Finally, when several windows are open at the same time, a lot of overhead can be expected on the device processor while switching between different windows during data acquisition.

This may slow down the loop that is performing data acquisition based on the capability of the device processor (Losavio *et al.*, 2003), (Moore, 2004).

5. EFFICIENCY

Historically, the terminology, classification, and structure of metrics and attributes applicable to software quality management have been extracted or derived from the ISO 9126-3 and the subsequent quality model ISO 25000:2005. Using these models, the Consortium for Information Technology Software Quality has provided five major characteristics desired for a piece of software to identify business value. They are efficiency, reliability, maintainability, security, and size. The efficiency of a mobile application is basically about performing the required actions efficiently. It can be measured by testing the codes and resources required by a program to perform a particular task or a specific function. The efficiency test of a mobile application is the number of test cases executed divided by the unit of time. Test effectiveness of mobile application covers three aspects:

1. The number of requirements of the users that are satisfied by the application,
2. To what extent the specifications of the users are achieved by the application, and
3. The amount of effort it takes to develop a particular application.

Thus, efficiency is closely related to the extent to which a process or a product can operate using the fewest possible resources. This is very important to mobile users to reduce the application's running cost, as it is a part of application quality (External mobile application quality) and constrained by software architecture. As with other quality attributes, cases of inefficiency in performance are often found in violation of coding practice in good architectural design. This can be detected by measuring the use of static quality attributes of the mobile application. These static quality attributes predict the possible bottlenecks in operational performance and problems of future scalability, particularly for mobile applications that demand high-speed execution for handling huge volumes of data or complex algorithms.

Assessing the efficiency of mobile application requires checking best practices of software application and technical attributes like coding practices, application architecture practices, data management, data access performance, interaction appropriate with expensive and/or remote resources, network, memory and disk space management, compliance with structured object-oriented programming best practices. A mobile application is efficient if it provides an equivalent or better result when compared to any alternative. The true reusability of objects and application of the black box concept, true elegant/clever programming techniques, and truly taking advantage of the current lowering of the cost of memory and hard disks (Lech, 2007), (Bohnet and Dollner, 2011), (Gary, 2011).

6. INTEROPERABILITY

The term interoperability is used to describe the ability of the application to work on different devices and platforms. In other words, two or more components of mobile applications can exchange information. Interoperability can be classified into different levels such as total interoperability, partial interoperability, and no interoperability.

- Total interoperability is when all the components of the application collaborate with other components. This is the most preferable level of Interoperability but difficult to achieve;
- Partial interoperability is when there is a collaboration between different components of the application;
- No interoperability when there is no collaboration whatsoever between components of the application (Ferrucci *et al.*, 2006), (Ke-Qing *et al.*, 2010).

The interoperability in the mobile industry is concerned with many questions such as:

- Should the mobile application be built for one operating system? Or
- Should it be developed only for the two big operating systems iOS and Android?
- If so, should developers build the applications simultaneously? And
- Should the application be designed as one application for both or two different applications for the two different platforms?
- How will the application be tested for many different Android options? or
- Should they use the Web *via* HTML5?

Pure interoperability of a mobile application is not technically possible as interoperability should consider many factors such as cultural, regional, lingual, and preferred user experiences or devices as well as the fact that every mobile device has its specifications. In short, there are different reasons to build different versions of an application for different groups of users, devices, and platforms. Developing interoperability for the Android platform faces another challenge called fragmentation within the operating system.

Fragmentation is a big issue on all mobile platforms as it forces mobile developers to code for different versions of the operating system and different devices that use the operating system. But this challenge is more pronounced in the Android operating system. Another obstacle to interoperability in the mobile application is that there are users who own different mobile devices and want to use them all in several circumstances. For example, one user may want to access a mobile application on a smartphone; another may prefer the same application on a tablet, and laptops as well (Holzinger *et al.*, 2012).

Building application that largely runs on an internal device but connects to the Web for specific tasks similar across different platforms. The objective of these hybrid applications is to save resources and time when possible while improving and optimizing the mobile application products for different operating systems. Google focuses on updating a series of applications aimed at improving interoperability (David and Yat, 2011), (Alin, 2012).

7. CONCURRENCY

Concurrency in mobile computing means a collection of mechanisms and techniques that enable a mobile application to perform several tasks simultaneously. Concurrency is about performing multiple parallel tasks using the mobile application and run at the same time as other application processes. In real life, many things are happening simultaneously at a particular time. Generally, there are two aspects when dealing with concurrency issues in mobile systems such as the ability to detect external events that occur in random order and ensure that these events are responded to in some minimum required interval. The main issues in developing concurrent mobile systems generally arise because of the interactions between concurrent activities. Thus when interactions happen between concurrent activities, some kind of coordination is required. Another challenge is that mobile platform makes concurrent programming similar to what used to be called real-time computing or real-time programming, (Software Corporation, 2002).

The operating system of any mobile device (*e.g.*, Android, iOS, Windows… *etc.*) has a feature of concurrency to allows users to do several different tasks simultaneously and/or to enable several different users to access the same mobile device at the same time. Many mobile operating systems enable many tasks to run simultaneously and use peripheral devices concurrently. The earliest use of concurrency in mobile computing was in real-time systems such as mobile operating systems, in which the applications perform a specific action determined by external events at a specific time (Axford, 2002). Most programming languages are inherently sequential where the processor performs one single instruction at a time. Achieving substantial concurrency in a mobile application is easy using multiple processors, but as interactions become more complex, communication between application tasks running on different processors is the main concern.

Generally, there are different layers of mobile application involved that add timing overhead and increase the complexity of the application. Mobile device users may simultaneously listen to music, use a web browser, or send/receive text messages or voice calls, or take directions from a navigator. The nature of concurrent demands put on operating systems and mobile applications has changed by mobile appliances. Finally, concurrency in a mobile application can be more difficult to understand because they lack a specific state in the mobile system. The state of a concurrent mobile system is the aggregate of the states of the system components (Meike, 2014).

8. DATA AGNOSTICISM

Agnosticism, in a mobile computing context, refers to the generalization that it is interoperable between different mobile computing systems. The term not only refers to mobile software and hardware applications but also mobile business processes or practices. Generally, agnosticism can refer to the ability of mobile software or hardware application to function with various mobile systems, rather than being customized to a single target system.

Agnosticism can be translated to the ability to function without knowing the details of a mobile computing system that is working within. Similar to interoperability, agnosticism is normally enabled by either compliance with broadly used standards or added components (*i.e.* coding) which allows one mobile computing system to function in multiple computing environments. There are four existing types of agnosticism in mobile computing such as:

1. Platform-agnosticism refers to the fact that a mobile application can run on any combination of a mobile operating system and the underlying architecture of the processor. Such mobile applications are called cross-platform applications.
2. Device-agnosticism refers to mobile application operations on different types of devices, including smartphones, tablets, laptops, and PCs.
3. Data-agnosticism refers to a mobile application's ability to function with a different vendor's database management system (DBMS).
4. Protocol-agnosticism refers to that the mobile application is independent of communication protocols.

A business process-agnostic mobile application can function in various business environments. Data-agnosticism describes the capacity of a mobile application to operate with any database management system (DBMS). A data-agnostic mobile software application can be useful in different environments in which data must be obtained from heterogeneous databases. Nevertheless, a data-agnostic product is not customized to the function with a specific DBMS, it normally cannot get an advantage from any special feature that the mobile system provides.

Moreover, data agnosticism can also be affected by platform agnosticism as it is concerned with the design philosophies and attributes of mobile application products. A mobile platform-agnostic application functions equally well across more than one mobile platform. In case a mobile platform-agnostic application is used, the mobile platform must be specified with a more detailed justification. When referring to a mobile application product, platforms normally refer to common mobile operating systems (OS), like Apple's iOS, Google's Android, Windows Phone... *etc*. Device agnosticism is one of the key factors that can affect the capacity of mobile computing components to function with numerous mobile systems without any special adaptations (Janssen, 2010), (Margaret, 2011).

9. EXTENSIBILITY

Generally in information technology and particularly in mobile computing, extensibility refers to some feature such as a program, a protocol, or a programming language that is designed to enable mobile users or developers to add or expand its application capabilities. Mobile application needs to be designed and developed with the goal of extensibility to avoid application code rot. Extensibility can be defined as the ability of a mobile application to be extended with new or updated functionality with a slight or no effect on the flow of data at the same time, maintain internal structure intact.

Extensibility is one of the main features that contribute to quality attributes of capability in a mobile application. To achieve extensibility completely, the design of a mobile application has to consider three features in the application namely: modifiability, maintainability, and scalability. Modifiability can be defined as the smallest amount of change to the least number of elements. Maintainability is similar to modifiability as it is about designing a mobile system that allows the addition of extra requirements with no risk of new errors. Maintainability and modifiability are used to complement each other rather than serve the same purpose. Scalability is the ability of the mobile system to expand in a selected dimension without major changes to its architecture. Many other quality attributes are useful for application extensibility in some way; however, the identified quality attributes are the primary attributes that influence extensibility (Johansson, 2009).

A common mobile platform integrates a heterogeneous distributed environment and simplifies communications, code-data mobility, and replication. Mobile application code is concerned with the service of mobile user requests rather than distribution. Facilitating mobile system extension and customization gives mobile developers the flexibility to easily make or change deployment options. For this purpose, mobile developers need a flexible mobile system that enables them to easily build and modify distributed application deployments with no need to rewrite major parts of their mobile application. In general, earlier or existing distributed programming systems are not created for general-purpose, extensible, or flexible enough to support mobile application requirements. Therefore, designing any mobile applications has to consider and explore customizability and extensibility in certain contexts such as operating systems, distributed storage, databases, and routers, and switches (Zhang, 2014). Thus, mobile application extensibility is an important attribute as it enables developers or third parties to change behavior, add features, and/or develop a customized user interface for the mobile devices used in warehouse operations.

SUMMARY

The present chapter has discussed the capability features of the mobile application as one of the main qualitative characteristics of a mobile application. This chapter is divided into seven sections where each section describes different sub-quality characteristic features. Section 1.3 has discussed mobile application completeness and section 1.4 has explored mobile application accuracy. Section 1.5 has discussed how the application efficiently performs its actions and section 1.6 has focused on the different features that interact with each other. Section 1.7 has discussed the application of multiple parallel tasks and section 1.8 has focused on possible data formats. Finally, section 1.9 has discussed the ability to add features or change the current behavior.

REFERENCES

Alin, Z. (2012). Integrability and interoperability of mobile applications. *Informatica Ec 150 Economica, 16*(4), 150-158.

Axford, T. (2002). Concurrency in software engineering. *Encyclopedia of Software Engineering.*

Bohnet, J., Dollner, J. (2011). Monitoring code quality and development activity by software maps. *Proceedings of the IEEE ACM ICSE Workshop on Managing Technical Debt,* 9-16. [http://dx.doi.org/10.1145/1985362.1985365]

David, K., Yat, S. (2011). The challenge of cross platform development.*The application developer alliance Emerging Tech Working Group.* Rocket Farm.

Ferrucci, D., Lally, A., Gruhl, D., Epstein, E., Schor, M., Murdock, W., Frenkiel, A., Brown, E., Hampp, T., Doganata, Y., Welty, C., Amini, L., Kofman, G., Kozakov, L., Mass, Y. (2006). *Towards an interoperability standard for text and multi-modal analytics. Technical report.* IBM RESEARCH.

Gary, G. (2011). Measuring software process. *In Process-Fusion.net.*

Holzinger, A., Treitler, P., Slany, W. (2012). Making apps useable on multiple different mobile platforms: On interoperability for business application development on smartphones. Multidisciplinary Research and Practice for Information Systems. *Lect. Notes Comput. Sci, 7465,* 176-189. [http://dx.doi.org/10.1007/978-3-642-32498-7_14]

Janssen, C. (2010). *Platform agnostic. Technical report.* TechOpedia.

Johansson, N., Lofgren, A. (2009). Designing for extensibility: An action research study of maximizing extensibility by means of design principles. *Master's thesis, University of Gothenburg, Department of Applied Information Technology, Gothenburg, Sweden.*

Ke-Qing, H., Wang, J., Liang, P. (2010). Semantic interoperability aggregation in service requirements refinement. *J. Comput. Sci. Technol, 25*(6), 1103-1117. [http://dx.doi.org/10.1007/s11390-010-9392-3]

Lech, M., Lukasz, S. (2007). Impact of aspect-oriented programming on software development efficiency and design quality: an empirical study. *IET Software Journal, 5*(1), 180-187.

Losavio, F., Ledis, C., Nicole, L. (2003). Quality characteristics for software architecture. *J. Object Technol, 2*(2), 133-150. [http://dx.doi.org/10.5381/jot.2003.2.2.a2]

Margaret, R. (2007). Functional specification. *In TechTarget – Sereach Software Quality.*

Margaret, R. (2011). database-agnostic *Technical report, TechTaget Search Data Management.*

Meike, G. (2014). *Concurrency in Android. Technical Report.* Thestrageloop.

Moore, D. (2004). Precision and accuracy in software. *In mooreds.com.*

Software Corporation. (2002). *Concepts. Concurrency. Technical report.* Rational Unified Process.

Zhang, I., Szekeres, A., Aken, D., Ackerman, I., Steven, D., Krishnamurthy, A., Henry, L. (2014). Customizable and extensible deployment for mobile/cloud applications. *11th USENIX Symposium on Operating Systems Design and Implementation,* 97-112.

CHAPTER 2

Reliability: Can a Mobile Application be Trusted in Many and Difficult Situations?

Abstract: This chapter discusses the reliability of a mobile application as one of the main quality attributes. This chapter considers the stability of a mobile application in terms of providing a mobile application without errors in the script or unhandled exceptions, or any other types of crashes. The focus is on the ability of a mobile application to discover, adapt, prevent, and recover from any mobile operational issues. This chapter emphasizes the possibility of the mobile operation to recover after any fatal mistake and continue to use the same mobile application even after a serious problem. Besides, it focuses on data integrity and discusses different behavioral issues of the application, such as predictability, consistency, and trustworthiness.

Keywords: Behavioral Issues, Consistency, Data Integrity, Fatal Mistake, Mobile Application, Operational Issues, Predictability, Qualitative Characteristics, Reliability, Stability, Trustworthiness.

1. INTRODUCTION

The present chapter discusses the reliability of a mobile application as one of the main quality attributes. This chapter is divided into seven sections. Section 2.1 is the introduction, leading to the graphic representation in the next section 2.2. Further, section 2.3 discusses the stability of a mobile application in terms of providing a mobile application without errors in the script or unhandled exceptions, or any other types of crashes. Section 2.4 focuses on the ability of a mobile application to discover, adapt, prevent, and recover from any mobile operational issues. Section 2.5 discusses the possibility of the mobile operation recovering after any fatal mistake and continue to use the same mobile application even after a serious problem. Section 2.6 focuses on data integrity. It keeps all types of data intact throughout the application. Section 2.7 discusses behavioral issues of the application, such as predictability, consistency, and trustworthiness.

Mohamed Sarrab, Hafedh Al-Shihi and Naveen Safia

2. RELIABILITY

Reliability in a mobile application is about the trust of the final product in many different situations as well as difficult situations. The reliability of a mobile application can be measured through features such as stability, robustness, stress handling, recoverability, data integrity, safety, disaster recovery, and trustworthiness. Fig. (2) presents the mobile application reliability factors.

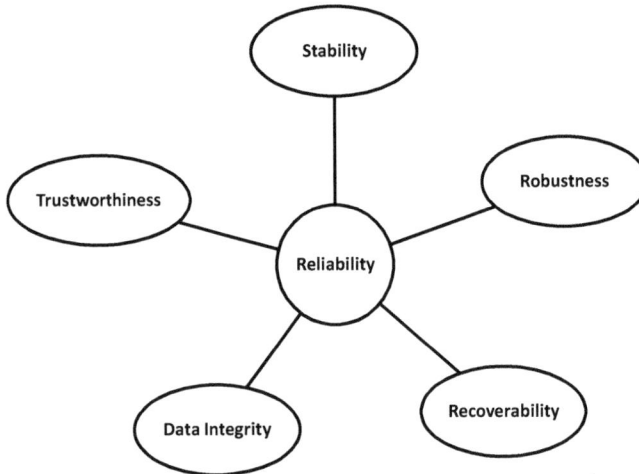

Fig. (2). Mobile Application Reliability Factors.

Stability refers to the ability of the final product to perform without crashes, script errors, or any exceptional problems that the mobile application cannot handle. Robustness refers to the ability to handle anticipated as well as unanticipated errors gracefully in the application. Recoverability is about the possibility of being able to recover and continue using the mobile application after a fatal error. Data integrity is defined as keeping all types of data intact in the product throughout the application. Trustworthiness refers to the application's behavior, such as predictability, consistency, and trustworthiness.

3. STABILITY

Stability in mobile computing focuses on the performance of the final product without crashes, script errors, and unhandled exceptions. Mobile application stability is about verifying the steadiness of the application in terms of its performance. In other words, it is about performing many software and hardware tasks over a period of time without the application getting locked, crashing, or restarting. A mobile application can crash during installing, executing, or launching. Any exceptions may occur due to some specific features of the device not being able to fit with the executed mobile application.

The main reason causing the application to crash during installation is that the mobile computing device capabilities may not support a particular mobile application requirement. This can occur because the application requests more resources than the device capability, or it can occur because a wrong application release has been downloaded (version) or platform. However, a native mobile application that is developed for a specific device normally runs without any problem.

A mobile application may crash during execution because the exceptions are not handled properly. If all possible exceptions are not specified and handled as part of the application development, it might lead to a crash when any user performs instructions that aggravate the exception. The best approach to solve exceptional issues is to list all exceptions as nonfunctional requirements and use clear coding guidelines to ensure that all the said functions have their exceptional handling routines. An exception testing procedure will help to ensure that all possible exceptions are covered before real-time use.

A mobile application may crash while launching due to inadequate resources in the device and corrupt cache from the previous launch. These issues can be fixed easily using real testing of mobile devices. Real and on-time device testing helps to specify the issues that can lead to a crash while launching (Jithesh *et al.*, 2012).

In 2014, a study was conducted by Ian to observe application behavior in the latest versions of the most common mobile operating systems: iOS and Android. It was found that the Google operating system was the most stable platform of all the available operating systems. This study investigated by measuring the application crash rate across both operating systems with a huge sample size of one billion mobile users for one month. But it dismissed the stigma that iOS applications are the most stable. While iOS versions 6, 7.0, and 7.1 had an application crash-rate of 2.5%, 2.1%, and 1.7% respectively, different releases in Google performed better across the board as Android 2.3 has 1.7% crash rate, and other released versions since 4.0 got just 0.7% application crash rates (Ian, 2014).

4. ROBUSTNESS

Robustness is one of the key quality attributes of any software which is defined by the IEEE standard as the degree of the correct function of a software system or component with the existence of stressful environmental conditions or invalid inputs (Arcuri and Briand, 2011), (Shahrokni and Feldt, 2013). The term, robust as an adjective, is usually applied to information technology products in different ways. A robust mobile application means that the application does not break easily. Thus, mobile OS in which an application can fail without disturbing the OS or other applications can be termed a robust application. Sometimes robust is also used to refer to a mobile system or an application product that is designed with a full range of capabilities. In a business context, early Palm OS and Bada systems were not considered as robust as Android and iOS. They were designed for continuous operation with a low failure rate and features that automatically back up file systems (Kevin and Margaret, 2005).

Hence, robustness in a mobile application is the ability of an application to detect, prevent, adapt, and recover from any operational problems. A mobile application is considered robust if it can tolerate any operational issues as invalid inputs, unavailable databases; corrupted internally, stressed overloads, unanticipated events, and improper uses, and so on. Since these operational issues can occur and they do occur in real-time operation, it is very important to test the robustness of the application to evaluate the ability of the application to handle different types of problems. Such tests intentionally make an application fail, to observe the behavior of the application (Collard, 2005).

Robustness in mobile computing can be used to describe one or more attributes such as a wide range of capabilities, quick recovery, not break down easily, hold up well under exceptional conditions, not wholly affected by a single application failure, or not wholly affected by a bug. However, it is worth noticing that application robustness on the most popular mobile platforms iOS and Android is continuously improved as a new version is released. For example, Apple iOS 8.0 had many problems, so new versions have been upgraded to deal with these issues and improve the robustness of the iOS platform. It is the same with Android OS variants. Quickly after 4.4, Google rolled out 4.4.2 (4.4.1 for Nexus only). Most of the mobile application developers have experienced all these recently developed great features and improvements that iOS and Android have continuously upgraded in every new version. These developers understand the importance of robustness across all the mobile devices used. Therefore, it is essential to test an application on real devices before launching to make the application significantly more robust (Helppi, 2014).

5. RECOVERABILITY

The software environment in mobile devices is unpredictable and the variability of mobile computing environments presents different challenges that have a significant impact on the way a mobile device functions and in some cases, it might cause the mobile application to fail. These issues emphasize the need to consider recoverability as the possibility to recover and continue using the mobile application after a fatal error or the mobile application's ability to come back to the normal function after a failure. The different failure scenarios include an unexpected power-down in which the application tester needs to validate the restarting process of the application to verify whether the application restarts properly and to check if the application settings and data are retained. A recovery process in mobile computing is used for handling failures in mobile systems. In a mobile computing environment, there are two different types of failures: voluntary and involuntary failures. The first type of failure is voluntary, where voluntary system interruptions intentionally give the system a chance to save its crucial state and data. The second is involuntary failures, which can occur at any time, and its source might be software or hardware issues. Involuntary failures can be handled by saving system snapshot as a checkpoint periodically and back to the previous system state (Kucuk, 1998).

Many automated testing tools can be used by the tester to test mobile applications. These testing tools can automate the testing process on virtualized devices, mobile emulators, and physical devices for mobile computing. Various testing tools can also replicate particular software/hardware conditions *i.e.* network connectivity, low battery, battery failure … *etc.* to test the amount of recoverability in a mobile application. Virtualized mobile devices are several third-party firms that offer remote-controllable access to different mobile devices through the cloud. Mobile emulators are of three different types: device emulators, browser emulators, and operating system emulators. These tools record the user interactions and play them back to measure actual and expected actions and results (KPMG, 2014).

The recovery of mobile application enables an application to perform clean up and data recovery operations *i.e.* capture the state of the application and releasing the used resources before shutting down. Mobile application recovery can improve the mobile end-user experience after an application crash. In case a fatal error occurs, a mobile application can use a recovery process to persist application state and data information before termination. So that it can automatically restarting the application to its previous state (MSDN, 2015). The ability to recover quickly from a mobile application failure depends not only on particular application and data backups but also on a predefined policy and plan for recovering that particular application setting and data to the previous state. The efficient and fast recovery process may include creating database back-ups, maintaining software records as well as hardware records. Thus any recovery plan should have these elements to ensure the application's ability to restore the deployment in the event of a failure of an application (FCS, 2009), (Miraclin and Thanushkodi, 2009).

6. DATA INTEGRITY

Data integrity in mobile computing deals with maintaining and assuring the accuracy and consistency of overall storage data. Data integrity is a fundamental quality characteristic for reliable a mobile application. Reliable access to different types of data is a prerequisite for most mobile applications. There are different reasons for any unauthorized or unexpected modifications of stored data as data can get corrupted due to software or hardware malfunctions (Prabhakaran *et al.*, 2005). Integrity violations can be caused by malicious intrusions and the detection of integrity violations is very important in ensuring the safety and reliability of the stored data. There are several types of data integrity in storage. The consistency of file system is one of the common types of integrity in storage, whereas most of the current file systems use integrity checking which scans the storage device to repair any logical inconsistencies between data and meta-data. This reduces the possibility of wasted disk space and file corruption in case a system crashes. Inconsistency of a file system can cause corruption of the data, although it might not usually cause security issues; system crash may make data files inaccessible due to inconsistency between the data and meta-data (Kim and Spafford, 1994).

Data access using mobile applications is constrained by unreliable hardware or software used. When designing mobile application data access, data storage designers should consider high latency, level of bandwidth, and intermittent connectivity, which directly affect the design of the application data storage. Designing access to data should consider mobile programming for data integrity as power failures may cause data integrity issues and data files that remain open during a mobile device suspension, especially when that data is stored on a removable storage device such as an SD memory card. Moreover, storage designers should consider using transactions with SQL Server Mobile to ensure data integrity in mobile systems in those cases where the mobile device loses connectivity or power (Meier *et al.*, 2009). Storage designers of mobile applications have to address integrity violations in file data as part of the file system inconsistencies. Integrity violations can also be caused by errors made by the users inadvertently or malicious activities. In most mobile systems that do not use integrity assurance mechanisms, stored data might be modified and passed undetected, or might be properly handled by the running mobile application. As a result, the stored data or cause the application to crash (Barlett and Spainbower, 2004), (Sivathanu and Zadok, 2005).

Currently, many mobile users store their data in the cloud, so the correctness of data integrity is a prime concern to ensure the security and integrity of data storage in the cloud (Alzahrani *et al.*, 2014). Consequently, data storage designers should ensure that the stored data of mobile users in the cloud is intact and data integrity is maintained (Sowparnika and Dheenadayalu, 2013).

7. TRUSTWORTHINESS

Trustworthiness in a mobile application is the overall character and measuring the behavior patterns of the mobile system, and comprehensively considering the characteristic attributes of security, safety, and tolerance to a fault and so on (Pranata *et al.*, 2013). Most of the mobile applications have a defect in the programmed code, which may cause the application to fail. With a huge number of mobile applications that appear in the application stores, in particular those that provide similar functions, mobile users are often confused with the selection of trustworthiness and high-quality mobile applications. The trustworthiness of a mobile application indicates that is appropriately free from these defects. Although a mobile application performs as specified, when it is needed and how it should, there is no mobile application at present that can be proven completely free of all defects. However, the level of trustworthiness of the application should be proper for the purpose for which the mobile application is used. This can be achieved by considering many key aspects such as safety, availability, security, and resilience, which together provide a trustworthy mobile application. Each of these aspects is needed to some degree according to the purpose of the application (Burton, 2013).

Trustworthiness is usually derived from the reputation of the application. Many different factors such as difficulty to find other users that have used the same mobile applications, different levels of satisfaction as the perception of each user is different about the type of quality, security, privacy level, *etc*. Dishonesty in reporting feedback is yet another factor because the rate providers may be malicious or dishonest in providing rating feedbacks. Rate incentives are also a very important factor as some application providers offer different types of incentives to users to give their positive rating. Therefore, feedback is used to build a successful reputation of trust. Several popular and prominent application stores such as Android Google Play and Apple Apps stores suffer from the above-mentioned issues. From these issues, initial trustworthiness is critical to be measured as users continually tend to choose the mobile application that has a good level of quality (Pranata *et al.*, 2013). Currently, there is a need to conduct in-depth research to provide solutions for measuring the trustworthiness of mobile applications before downloading or using them. The root cause of many issues is untrustworthy mobile applications, which are caused by vulnerabilities relating to safety, availability, resilience, security, and reliability in general. Therefore, there is an urgent and pressing need to address the reliability of our mobile software application in general to establish its consistency and trustworthiness (Kamthan, 2009), (Burton, 2013).

SUMMARY

This chapter has discussed the reliability of a mobile application and its sub-quality characteristics. It has introduced reliability in mobile applications. This chapter is divided into seven sections; each section has described different sub-quality characteristics. Section 2.1 has provided an introduction, leading to the graphic representation in the next section 2.2. Further, Section 2.3 has explored the stability of the mobile application concerning crashes, script errors, and unhandled exceptions. Section 2.4 has discussed the ability of a mobile application to detect, prevent, and recover from any problem due to any operation. Section 2.5 has focused on the possibility to recover and continue using the mobile application after serious errors or issues. Section 2.6 has described data integrity and has to keep all types of data intact throughout. Section 2.7 has focused on the behavior of the application whether the application is predictable, consistent, and trustworthy.

REFERENCES

Alzahrani, A., Alalwan, N., Sarrab, M. (2014). Mobile Cloud Computing: Advantage, Disadvantage and Open Challenge, Proceedings of the 7th Euro American on Telematics and Information Systems *ACM. Valparaiso, Chile.*

Arcuri, A., Briand, L. (2011). A practical guide for using statistical tests to assess randomized algorithms in software engineering. *33rd International Conference on Software Engineering (ICSE),* 1-10. [http://dx.doi.org/10.1145/1985793.1985795]

Barlett, W., Spainbower, L. (2004). Commercial fault tolerance: A tale of two systems. *Proceedings of the IEEE Transactions on Dependable and Secure Computing,* 87-96.

Burton, E. (2013). *Making Software Better, What is Trustworthy Software? Trustworthy Software Initiative.* TSI.

Collard, R. (2005). Verifying software robustness. *Workshop on Performance and Reliability (WOPR).*

FCS. (2009). *Recoverability.* Microsoft, USA: Forefront Client Security.

Helppi, V. (2014). *What every app developer should know about android. Technical report.* SMASHINGMAGAZINE.

Ian, A. (2014). Android apps twice as stable as ios ones, study shows.

Jithesh, S., Anoop, N., Navin, N., Shibu, K. (2012). A Comprehensive Guide to Enterprise Mobility. *(Infosys Press) Publisher: CRC Press, 1st edition.*

Kamthan, P. (2009). Computing: Concepts, Methodologies, Tools, and Applications, chapter addressing the Credibility of Mobile Applications *IGI Global*

Kevin, C., Margaret, R. (2005). Robust, whatis.techtarget. *techtarget.*

Kim, G., Spafford, E. (1994). Experiences with tripwire: Using integrity checkers for intrusion detection. *In Proceedings of the Usenix System Administration Networking and Security (SANS III).*

KPMG. (2014). *Addressing mobile applications risk: A software quality focus. Technical report.* KPMG LLP, Swiss.

Kucuk, G. (1998). *An application service provider for a mobile computing environment.*

Meier, J., Hill, D. (2009). Designing Mobile Applications. *Microsoft.*

Miraclin, J., Thanushkodi, K. (2009). Log management support for recovery in mobile computing environment. *(IJCSIS). Int. J. Comput. Sci. Inf. Secur,* 3(1)

MSDN. (2015). *Understanding Application Recovery and Restart.* USA: Microsoft.

Prabhakaran, V., Agrawal, N., Bairavasundaram, L., Gunawi, H., Arpaci-Dusseau, A., Arpaci-Dusseau, A. (2005). Iron file sysetms. In Proceedings of the 20th ACM Symposium on Operating Systems Principles (SOSP '05) *Brighton, UK,.*

Pranata, I., Athauda, R., Skinner, G. (2013). Determining trustworthiness and quality of mobile applications mobile wireless middleware, operating systems, and applications. *Lecture Notes of the Institute for Computer Sciences. Social Informatics and Telecommunications Engineering,* 65, 92-206.

Shahrokni, A., Feldt, R. (2013). A systematic review of software robustness. *Symposium on Search Based Software Engineering,* 1-17.

Sivathanu, G., Zadok, E. (2005). Ensuring data integrity in storage: Techniques and applications, stony brook university. *In Appears in the proceedings of the First ACM Workshop on Storage Security and Survivability* (StorageSS 2005), Sowparnika, M., & Dheenadayalu, R. (2013). Improving data integrity on cloud storage service. *International Journal of Engineering Science Invention,* 2(2), 49-55.

CHAPTER 3

Usability: Can Mobile Applications Be Used Easily?

Abstract: This chapter discusses the usability of a mobile application as one of the main qualitative attributes. The chapter focuses on the users' expectations about usability and the redundancy of content or appearance of the product. It discusses how fast and easy it to learn the use of the mobile application is by memorizing what has been learned from the application. Moreover, it emphasizes the application's capabilities to recover the required information. It discusses how experienced mobile users can perform common tasks very fast and the possibilities of interacting with other applications. This chapter emphasizes protection against making mistakes and meeting the accessibility standards, which apply to the mobile application.

Keywords: Capabilities, Easy to Learn, Experienced Mobile Users, Interaction, Mobile Application, Qualitative Characteristics, Redundancy, Usability, Users' Expectation.

1. INTRODUCTION

This chapter focuses on the usability of a mobile application as one of the main qualitative attributes. This chapter is divided into fifteen sections. The chapter begins with an introduction, Section 3.1, followed by a pictorial representation of the sub-themes of usability in section 3.2. These sub-themes will be discussed in the following sub-sections. Section 3.3 discusses the users' expectations about usability. Section 3.4 focuses on the redundancy of content or appearance of the product. Section 3.5 discusses how fast and easy to learn the use of the mobile application is. Section 3.6 focuses on the memorization ability of what has been learned from the mobile application. Section 3.7 focuses on the application capabilities and information that can be discovered. Section 3.8 discusses how experienced mobile users can perform common tasks very fast. Section 3.9 focuses on the possibilities of interacting with other applications. Section 3.10 discusses the feelings of users in control over the proceedings of the mobile application. Section 3.11 focuses on the use of clear language with an emphasis on understanding easily. Section 3.12 focuses on protection against making mistakes. Section 3.13 discusses the behavior of the application. Section 3.14

Mohamed Sarrab, Hafedh Al-Shihi and Naveen Safia

focuses on meeting the accessibility standards, which are applicable to the mobile application. Finally, section 3.15 discusses how to provide the help function for users and match the functions with the application.

2. USABILITY

Complex mobile applications have found their way into the modern lives of users. As a consequence, mobile developers can see the benefits of designing and developing their applications from the user perspective rather than technology-oriented methods. The main attributes which reflect the usability of a mobile application are intuitiveness, minimalism, learnability, memorability, discoverability, operability, interactivity, control, clarity, errors, consistency, accessibility, and documentation. As illustrated in Fig. (**3**), Mobile Application Usability Factors

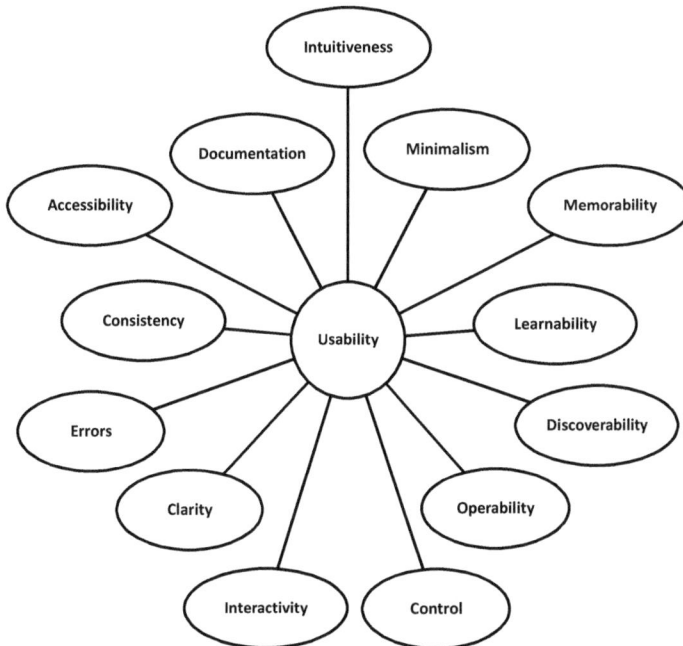

Fig. (3). Mobile Application Usability Factors.

The intuitive mobile application considers the expectations of users, such as having a user-friendly interface. Minimalism is all about the redundancy in the content or appearance of the product. Learnability considers how fast or easy it is for the learner to learn the use of the mobile application. Memorability focuses on the ability to remember what is learned from using the mobile application.

Discoverability focuses on the application's capabilities and information that can be discovered by exploring the user interface. Operability deals with the speed at which experienced users can perform common tasks. Interactivity is about easy-to-understand possibilities of interacting with other applications. Control is about the user's feeling of being in control over the proceedings of the mobile application. Clarity is focused on explicitly stating every detail in clear language. Errors are about how difficult to make mistakes as well as fixing them easily if any mistakes occur. Consistency relates to behaving in the same way throughout the application. Accessibility focuses on meeting the accessibility standards that are applicable to mobile applications. Documentation is about providing help and matching with functionality.

Each of these qualitative attributes has an impact on the overall usability of the mobile application, which can be used to evaluate the usability feature of the application. Mobile devices that are small in size have limited ways to interact. Issues such as the limited input modalities, poor connectivity, and small screen size also affect the usability feature of mobile applications.

3. INTUITIVENESS

Intuitive mobile applications relate to the expectations of the users and have a user-friendly interface. Mobile applications are termed intuitive when the users understand the function of the application and behavior without any need for special training, experimentation, or assistance. For this level of intuition, mobile users require prior information, either from other mobile applications in use or from experience in the real world. For example, in the case of a hybrid link, users can click on it if they knew from their experience of using other mobile applications or software. Alternatively, in the case of a push button, users who know from the real world can click on it to perform some tasks or make something happen. Thus, intuitiveness in a mobile application can be broken down into two requirements: consistency and affordance.

Consistency is about making a correct prediction and affordance is about predicting what is going to happen based on appearance. Moreover, the mobile application is intuitive if it has an appropriate combination of expectation, efficiency, responsiveness, affordance, explorability, forgiveness and at the same time, it causes no frustration to the user. The functional expectation of the mobile application is that the mobile user interface delivers the predictable output and expected results, with no surprising incidents. These user expectations are based on real-world experiences. The efficiency of the mobile application relates to the user interface which enables the users to act with less effort although the clear intention is the user interface that delivers the user expected results the first time.

Therefore, users do not need to repeat the same action.

Responsiveness of the mobile application is about the user interface that gives immediate and clear feedback to indicate that an action is performed which is either achieved or unachieved (successful or unsuccessful). Affordance is mostly visual; the mobile user interface has clues that indicate what it is going to do. Forgiveness is when the right action is performed even when mobile users make a mistake or at least the wrong action is undone easily or can be fixed. Explorability of mobile refers to the ability of the users to navigate throughout the user interface of the application without getting lost or afraid of penalty or unintended consequences. When the users are emotionally satisfied with the interaction level, no frustration is caused at any stage.

Generally, if users cannot figure out how to access or use the mobile application, they blame the mobile application developers. Mobile users should keep in mind the fact that software in general and a mobile application, in particular, is often used to accomplish very complex tasks and solve some complex issues. The mobile application does not need to be intuitive to the users who do not know very much about the application. The value of intuitiveness in the mobile application depends on how frequently this application is used. Complex mobile tasks have complex mobile applications. But, mobile application developers need to keep finding ways to make sure that mobile users can fly on their own and speed up their performance (James, 2009), (McKay, 2010).

4. MINIMALISM

Mobile applications upgrade and extend the functions and capabilities of mobile devices constantly. Mobile devices are no longer for just voice calling or sending text messages. They are currently used for different purposes in their business, professional as well as personal lives. Due to lower computing power, lower resolutions, and smaller screens of mobile devices, it is necessary for mobile application developers to make use of a minimum of designs to optimize both the functionality and aesthetic aspects of the application. In mobile computing, minimalism refers to minimizing redundancy in content and appearance. The mobile application developers should always focus on finding out the presence of any irrelevant or redundant content and if there is a fine balance between the level of minimalism and the visibility feature of the mobile application.

Mobile applications are gradually becoming highly refined to such an extent that now applications focus on a single task rather than a single application that performs several functions. So mobile users have become more adept with the use of devices and more comfortable in replying through mobile applications.

Designing mobile applications as native apps, web apps, or hybrid apps relies on careful planning and great developments in the user interface. Some examples of successful mobile applications are simple, sleek, flat, minimal, and single-task applications.

A few available applications make it clear. Rubie is a mobile application game that has a simple layout and the graphics resemble those of a colorful mobile game. The sky is another colorful (color-filled?) mobile application with a very minimal interface. Timeful is a smart mobile application, which resembles a calendar that is used for scheduling user's activities with an overall super clean interface. Clear is a super minimalistic to-do list mobile application that helps users to stay organized. The minimalism of this application makes it successful by sorting out the user's tasks and priorities. Squarespace mobile application has a clean design style. TeuxDeux mobile application is used to create to-do lists on the mobile device as well as update users' lists on the desktop on a computer with virtually no graphics but with colored text on white background. Peek is a super colorful mobile application like a calendar with a non-traditional twist. Authentic Weather is a mobile application that provides accurate weather information with minimal design. Rise mobile application is a different kind of alarm clock application where the user interface and the overall design of the application are minimal. Facebook uses a grid layout that helps users to access various functions and services without getting confused (Borowska, 2014), (Babich, 2016).

The layout, design, and user interface are very important factors to build a successful mobile application. At the same time, the graphic and textual elements of the application are optimized. Therefore, mobile applications need to consider a minimalist concept in their designing approaches (Payne, 2007).

5. LEARNABILITY

According to ISO/IEC-9126-1; Learnability is a very important attribute of usability (ISO/IEC, 2006). Usability is known as a qualitative attribute that determines the ease of use provided by the user interface (Fetaji *et al.*, 2008), while learnability is the time needed to learn to use the application. Generally, it is well-accepted that learnability is one of the key aspects of usability, but there is little consensus among specialists on how learnability should be defined, evaluated, and measured. Due to this lack of consensus, it is not a surprise that mobile applications still challenge mobile users with learning difficulties (Grossman *et al.*, 2009). The assessment and importance of learnability as one of the usability attributes in a mobile application varies based on the type of users and applications.

Nielsen defines a system's learnability as a degree to which a system interface helps novice users to perform useful tasks (Nielsen, 1993) and develop expertise in using the system quickly. It can also be described as the ability of a user interface to allow mobile users to accomplish different tasks in the first attempt. Furthermore, learnability can be defined as the usability of the application over a period of time. A more learnable mobile application is the one that reduces the required time to complete the tasks as mobile users consume more time with an application that is faster than others. In some cases, a certain amount of training is required to learn how to use the application (Sauro, 2013).

The learnability of mobile applications is mainly affected by the design of the user interface. For example, some research studies have reported that mobile application user interfaces have too many icons on the menu, and the functions and the menu are difficult and very complicated to be understood (Kurniawan, 2007). These design-related complicated issues challenge the mobile application community to find the right way to improve the learnability of applications in mobile devices. Although different mobile technologies and facilities have great potential to support the current learning system, there are still several other existing mobile applications that are difficult to use. This may harm the wide adoption of these mobile technologies. So research is significantly in demand to improve the learnability of mobile applications for different levels of learners. Different approaches might be used to improve mobile application learnability and to help mobile developers to build successful mobile applications that are easier to use and adopt. Some examples are using multi-layered interfaces, improving graphical icons, and augmenting the mobile interface (Leung *et al.*, 2008), (Rock, 2011). To sum up, more research investigation is needed to improve and develop the learnability of the mobile application.

6. MEMORABILITY

Memorability of the mobile application refers to how quickly a user can pick up the required knowledge about the software application which he has not used for a while. Memorability is one of the usability attributes that considers the ease of memorizing the mobile application's functions in such a way that a casual mobile user can return to use the mobile application after a gap of not using, without any need for training or learning again how to use the application.

Acquired knowledge and information about the user interface metaphors, symbols, and expected action results have to be easy to recall without any need to repeat the learning process even though the user has lost touch with the application. A mobile application might not be used or operated regularly and sometimes it may be used rarely. Thus, it is necessary for mobile users to remember how to use the application without any need to retrain or relearn it after discontinuing its use for some time. Memorability can be measured by examining mobile application users to perform a sequence of tasks after becoming familiar with such an application and then examining the same users to perform similar tasks after a period of inactivity.

The main point is to measure how well mobile users can re-establish the required skill of using the application; As a consequence, the two sets of results can be compared to determine how memorable the mobile application is. Measuring mobile application usability based on these different attributes may be inappropriate because some criteria overlap others. For example, memorability is very much related to learnability. In a case where a mobile application product is easy to learn and understand, it can probably be efficiently memorized and quickly picked up even after not using for a substantial period (Holzinger, 2005), (Ferre *et al.*, 2001), (Seffah and Metzker, 2004).

Memorability of a mobile application is entirely dependent on the particular circumstances in which the mobile application is used. Some examples are the type of the users, the performed tasks and actions, and the social and physical environments in which they operate.

7. DISCOVERABILITY

The mobile system consists of application programs that control the operations of mobile and other linked devices. A mobile software application serves as the interface between a mobile user, application software, and hardware device. The software application is the operating system of the mobile. Even before operating the mobile application, the mobile OS must be loaded which comprises instructions to coordinate the actions for the mobile device to perform. The user interface controls the user inserted instructions or data and how information is presented and displayed on the mobile screen. Mobile applications have a graphical user interface that combines text, images, and other visual graphics to make the software application easier to use.

A mouse is a new interaction model used to point at things. It is a very huge jump for different reasons. First, instead of a couple of keyboard commands, a user interface designer could create menus and allow the user to discover the capabilities and functionalities of the software application. It can also be used to enable software users to move items from one place to another on the screen in an easily understood manner. Thus, for the first time, the user does not need to be a software expert to use the application as the software itself is user-friendly and offers a menu with a range of options to choose from. In the early 1970s, Xerox pushed the idea one step further and provided a graphical user interface, and came up with a desktop metaphor.

Discoverability of the mobile application is about the capabilities, functions, and other important information that can be discovered by exploring the designed user interface. The real advantage of Graphical User Interface (GUI) is that instructions and commands no longer need to be memorized. Instead, all possible operations with the designed interface could be discovered by mobile users through the systematic exploration of the menu provided. The discoverability of a mobile application is an important principle that has disappeared in most mobile phones. Apple developer team specifically recommends against the use of menu interfaces. However, Android developers recommend using menu interfaces and provide a dedicated menu key, although it does not always need to be active. It must be noted that the expectations of end users' are increasing regarding the usability of the mobile application. Therefore, the user interface needs to be well designed to provide a successful mobile application (Nielsen, 2010), (Norman, 2010).

8. OPERABILITY

In the context of mobile computing, operability is a measure of how well a mobile system operates while running. Simply it can be said that a mobile application with high operability works well and is operable. A good operable mobile application minimizes the effort and time required for unplanned interventions to keep the application running. Similarly, the mobile application with good operability anticipates and diagnoses errors. The mobile application with a high level of operability is easy to test and deploy in different mobile environments. A highly operable mobile application provides an experienced user with the right amount of good-quality information about the service provided (Skelton, 2015).

Operability in the mobile application is the ability of the application to interwork and cooperate in a given environment in such a way that experienced mobile users can perform common tasks very fast. In a mobile application platform, software applications and hardware proliferations must coexist successfully on different advanced mobile devices. A mobile application must not negatively affect the user by requiring actions and performance of the device or interfere with other processes or applications. Mobile users can perform the tasks needed in certain applications while other processes or applications are running simultaneously (KPMG, 2014).

Operability in the mobile application is influenced by mobility for interactive tasks such as navigation and data input. The limitations of mobile hardware such as smaller keyboards require more attention to perform the process or application tasks when navigating or inserting the data. However, the mobile surrounding environment also has an impact on the interaction process. The mobile user might be distracted when performing tasks in motion. Therefore, the speed, accuracy, and correctness of the input process may be lower (Spriestersbach and Springer, 2004).

9. INTERACTIVITY

In mobile computing, interactive computing refers to a mobile software application that simply accepts user input as data or commands. The nature of interactive mobile computing and its impact on mobile users are studied extensively in the human-computer interaction domain. Interactivity is about accepting mobile users' input. Interactive mobile applications are programs that support mobile users to insert data or commands. However, a non-interactive mobile program is a program that starts and continues without any user contact or interaction; for example, a mobile processor is a non-interactive program as it processes a mobile application.

Typically, a mobile application has several activities. Each activity displays a user interface that allows the user to perform a specific task such as taking a photo or viewing a map. Interaction in a mobile application is the collaboration between two or more components ArchiMate (2009). Interactivity is the dialogue that occurs between mobile users (or possibly another live creature) and a mobile software application. Therefore, mobile programs that are executed without immediate user involvement are not interactive. They are typically referred to as batch or background programs. Different mobile games are generally thought of as fostering a great level of interactivity. However, many other different business applications are also interactive, but in a more controlled manner that provides fewer options for user interaction (Margaret, 2011A).

An application program interface (API) is a set of protocols, tools, and routines that are used to build mobile software applications. The API specifies the mobile application components that will interact when programming the components of a graphical user interface (GUI). There are different types of application program interfaces for applications, websites, or operating systems; for example, when we copy and paste texts from one mobile application to another, it is the application program interfaces that allow this type of action to be performed successfully. Most mobile operating environments provide an application program interface so that application developers can develop applications consistent with the operating environment. Currently, application program interfaces are also specified by websites such as eBay or Amazon that allow developers to create specialized web stores using the existing retail infrastructure. Third-party mobile application developers also use web application program interfaces to create mobile application solutions for mobile users (Vangie, 2015).

10. CONTROL

Mobile phone users have distinctly different experiences with a mobile software application in which they are frustrated and feel a lack of control over the application used. So the mobile user interfaces should be created to help them that have highly positive experiences and can maintain control over different mobile activities. To quote a common example, lack of control while driving a car in traffic leads to an accident. Similarly, it is important that a mobile user feels in control of the application used (Kaptelinin, 1993), (Lee and Bederson, 2003), (Bederson, 2004).

The mobile user interface maintains control on how the user enters data or instructions and how information should be displayed on different mobile device screens. Most mobile applications available today use a graphical user interface. A graphical user interface (GUI) combines different interaction methods such as text, graphics, and other visual images to make the applications easier to use and control. Control features can prevent specified mobile applications from starting or blocking access to blacklisted websites as well as preventing access to the used components in the operating system. To a mobile user, control can permit access only to specified websites, and block unwanted websites where, users can also block only certain categories of unnecessary sites, such as online auctions, entertainment sites, or online games.

Users can set up filters that search and find specific expressions and block any websites on which they appear. They can also modify or update these filters at any time to add or delete existing keywords or websites. This approach maintains control over website access. Moreover, user control can completely block access to certain settings in a mobile system. Mobile users can specify which functions are available and start with menu options that are available through system/application setting control. The users can also change the appearance of the application items as well as limit the internet functions by changing the browser settings or preventing downloads. Furthermore, they can control or freeze the application item's appearance as they set it up. This may include the ability to move icons too (Salfeld, 2015).

11. CLARITY

An important issue in the quality of the mobile application is the measurement of programming style in the mobile application. Different techniques attempt to provide a quantitative equality assessment of several aspects that contribute to the quality of mobile applications. Currently, many experts are attempting to prepare application guidelines. If they are followed, users will have a positive effect of improving programming style in the mobile application. This kind of improvement will reduce the effort required to prepare a program and maintain or understand the resultant mobile product. In other words, to accurately evaluate mobile application programming style, it necessary to assess the amount of mental effort expended in understanding and preparing the used code for mobile application development.

Clarity and ease in understanding a particular mobile application program are influenced by three factors: structure, form, and developer's skills and ability. Some experiments were performed to assess the impact of program structure on the program's comprehensibility. The structure includes different factors related to the syntactic representation of an algorithm in the programming language used. For example, the complexity of the control flow graph in a mobile application program, the number of statements that can be executed, the clustering of data references, the depth of statement nesting, and the location of operations influence the mobile application structure and affect the overall application clarity. The developers' familiarity with the problem domain can strongly influence the clarity and ease with which a mobile application program is understood. This familiarity might enable application developers to recognize blocks of programming code very quickly as if a template matching operation had been mentally employed. Background information about the types of mobile applications in which developers work and achieve information used as a covariate should be collected. Thus, mobile application developers should avoid language inconsistencies including spelling errors (Ronald, 1978), (Alan *et al.*, 1981).

12. ERRORS

Some many issues and challenges that need to be considered in the development process of a mobile application. These challenges include some errors and mistakes that should be avoided when developing a mobile application. They are:

• User interface inconsistency
• Confusing browsing through the application
• Lack of clarity between graphics and text

- Hidden features that users do not know about and cannot find
- Language inconsistency and spelling errors
- Omission of the privacy policy
- Lack of help available to the application
- Application crashing without warning
- Distortion of screen orientation
- Lack of notification regarding network connectivity
- Information about error messages and
- Difficulty to repair errors

The worst of these errors and mistakes would crash the application without any warning or appropriate error message. The user interface has to be consistent throughout the application and software key references. The steps of browsing the application must be clear to the user with all unnecessary steps eliminated. All animations, graphics, and text material displayed should be clear and accessible to the user. The design of the application should not introduce any new feature that the user is unaware of.

The application must work in accordance with the associated help menu and display text information in the localized version of the application that is applicable and consistent throughout and must be free of spelling mistakes. The privacy and information flow policy should always be clear within the design of the application (Alshohoumi *et al.*, 2019). Help or assistance should always be available to the users and make sure that the application does not terminate or crash unexpectedly. The system that attempts to terminate the application due to a sudden lack of memory, storage, or connection should be monitored. The display of text information should not be distorted in case of changing from portrait or landscape modes. The developed application should be able to handle situations in case of weak or no network connection, loss, or delay in displaying the relevant and timely information to the application user. The application should have formative and expressive error messages.

Many different ways can lead developers to miss the mark when designing a mobile application or developing content design for mobile devices. Many organizations attempt to spread their customer service to the mobile platform market. This has led to the misconception that any successful application can also be a successful mobile application. The desktop developers and information technology leaders should not assume that, because mobile devices have their specifications, their applications, browsers, and content are developed for use by mobile devices. Thus, it is necessary to plan for content with products and services that are specifically suitable for the mobile platform. Otherwise, users will not use them with an indifferent or poor experience. In case they perform poorly, mobile solutions can very easily destroy user service reputation. Finally, the mobile application should be made in such a way that it is difficult to make mistakes and easy to repair (Faas, 2012).

13. CONSISTENCY

One of the important aspects in the development process of a mobile application is the consistency between different components of the mobile software application being designed and developed. In mobile application design, look and feel are two important characteristics, together termed as the graphical user interface. The way it looks refers to its design, involving different design elements such as layout, shapes, size, colors, and typefaces. The way it feels is determined by the behavior of dynamic elements, such as boxes, menu lists, and buttons. The development process of the mobile application should have a set of interface guidelines for different computing platforms to ensure that mobile application programs have a consistent look and feel (Heimdahl, 1996). It should be noted that in the field of mobile application designing, some designers try to re-create, re-invent, or even completely break the standard of hardware interactions with their interface patterns.

There are three types of consistencies that designers should consider to be effective. Mobile application designers should stay consistent with their design, with the device user interface behaviors and guidelines, and with other similar mobile applications.

Users do not want to go from the main page to a subpage and see different styling, colors, shapes, or any major or surprising different user interactions. Consistency is not only a big deal to the overall usability of the mobile application, but it can also greatly improve conversion as well. Therefore developers need to consider that the interaction and structure affect the overall mobile user experience. Moreover, it is very important to consider how to consistently place elements throughout the application. It is essential to think of the user interface patterns to be used, plan the type of input elements that are needed, find out the type of icons to be needed and design a good icon set that covers them all.

The design and style of each user interface component and maintaining consistency between them are important to the mobile user. The design of the user interface in a mobile application should consider the color scheme, type, and fonts, size, background image style, borders, and effects to create consistency (Monge*et al.*, 2002), (Lian *et al.*, 2008), (Patrick, 2012).

14. ACCESSIBILITY

Given a high degree of penetration, mobile communications are opening up new channels of doing businesses and mobile platform has become an ideal platform for delivering a wide range of applications and services. Improving the accessibility of mobile applications not only benefits the users with disabilities but also helps different organizations to fulfill their legal responsibility, widen client base, and build the corporate image. Opportunities arise for organizations to provide accessible applications on the mobile platform to take advantage of the fast-growing digital economy as well as harness innovation in technology. To build an accessible mobile application, the developers must specify accessibility requirements of mobile applications and the specialized needs of different segments of the community.

Developing a mobile application for a specialized group of users to access is the beginning of a new journey. It is a journey with no limits as the improvement in mobile platforms and technology applications generate new horizons. Therefore there is a possibility to develop mobile applications that are more easily accessible. At the same time, it poses many more challenges for accessibility. Developers should consider that there are many steps to improve mobile application accessibility. For example, developers should learn about accessibility and how disabled users may deal with the application. They should have quick accessibility check to get an estimate of how accessible the application is and develop a mobile user interface that is clear and easy to understand and operate.

Furthermore, they should publish an accessibility statement to express their intent to be accessible and provide easy step-by-step page navigation as simple as possible. They should also design an application that ensures text formatting to be altered by users to read a text, provide format using a theme and size that meets users' requirements. Finally, an application should be designed in such a way that it provides a "contact us" function that enables users to tell developers about any accessibility issues. These steps should significantly improve most mobile applications' accessibility concerns. But they are only the initial steps to successful accessibility practice. By this users can have an application that is more accessible and can also understand the benefits of accessibility. These steps are relevant to all mobile applications irrespective of the type, operating system, or hardware (OGCIO, 2018).

In general, mobile applications are covered by the same standards for access by disabled users that apply to non-mobile web or software applications. U.S. laws such as Section 508, the Americans with Disabilities Act (ADA), and the Twenty-First Century Communications and Video Accessibility Act (CVAA) can be applied in different ways. However, mobile applications including mobile web applications can be covered by one or more accessibility standards. Moreover, the guidelines of international standards for web content accessibility the WCAG 2 are a good basis to ensure that mobile applications are accessible to disabled users. The final mobile application product should be able to use by as many people as possible and should meet applicable international accessibility standards (Jonathan, 2013).

15. DOCUMENTATION

To use a mobile application on mobile devices, users need to have some helpful documentation prepared by those specialist technical writers who are generally behind the mobile application documentation and guidelines. The main focus of these technical writers is to write helpful documents that facilitate users to use the application, beginning with how to start the application, how to troubleshoot the application in case of bugs popping up, using 'help' or 'assist' to investigate concerns and issues before contacting customer support. The users also learn how to manage and adjust various settings according to their needs. These guidelines are available in various forms of help menus in the application, instructions, and online documents that the user can access once the application is purchased.

This technical writing document provides information on how the application is developed, how it functions, and how it can be accessed, manipulated, maintained, and extended to provide different functions. Thus, the documents are also helpful for higher-level application designers and users. The information that is required as a 'help' to use a mobile application needs to be part of the application menu options itself in different forms of labels, microcopies, and interaction language. The focus and flow of the application, mainly about how it operates and the design approach, especially including the language, has to be good enough so the users do not misunderstand or do not require content to be delivered beyond the application's context. The documents should act as a communication medium between the developing team and work as an information repository to be used by the maintenance team.

The document should provide information for management to help in planning, costing, and the agenda of the developmental process. Moreover, some of the documents should tell mobile users how to use, set up, and administer the application or the system. The documents are classified into two categories: product and process. The product documents describe the mobile application product that is being developed. It focuses on developing and maintaining the system from the developers' perspectives. The documents also deliver explanations geared towards the users. However, the process documents record the development process and maintenance. Moreover, the plans, schedules, organizational quality, and project standards are included in the process documentation (Dinga, 2014).

SUMMARY

This chapter has discussed the usability of a mobile application as one of its main qualitative attributes. It has provided an introduction to the usability of mobile applications. This chapter has been divided into fourteen sections, where each section describes a different sub-quality characteristic. Section 3.3 has discussed the users' usability expectation and section 3.4 has focused on the redundancy of product content or appearance. Section 3.5 has discussed how fast and easy to learn to use the mobile application and section 3.6 has focused on the memorization of what has been learned even when it is not used for a long period. Section 3.7 focuses on the capabilities of the application and information that can be discovered while section 3.8 discusses how experienced mobile users can perform common tasks very fast. Section 3.9 focuses on the possibilities of interacting with other applications. Section 3.10 discusses the users' feelings in control over the proceedings of the mobile application. Section 3.11 focuses on the use of clear language that can be easily understood. Section 3.12 focuses on the difficulty to make mistakes. Section 3.13 discusses the behavior of the application. Section 3.14 focuses on meeting the mobile application applicable accessibility standards. Finally, section 3.15 discusses how to provide help to the users and match the functions of the application.

REFERENCES

Alan, J, Frederick, S., Mary, S. (1981). Software Metrics: An Analysis and Evaluation. *MIT Press.*

Alshohoumi, F., Sarrab, M., Al-Abri, D., Al Hamadani, A. (2019). Systematic Review of Existing IoT Architectures Security and Privacy Issues and Concerns. *International Journal of Advanced Computer Science and Applications, 10*(7), 232-251. [IJACSA].
[http://dx.doi.org/10.14569/IJACSA.2019.0100733]

ArchiMate. (2009). *Archimate versi on 0.1 Specification.* The Open Group.

Babich, N. The Art of Minimalism in Mobile App UI Design *UX Planet.* https://uxplanet.org/

Bederson, B. (2004). Interfaces for staying in the flow.
[http://dx.doi.org/10.1145/1029383.1074069]

Borowska, P. (2014). 19 exceptionally well designed mobile app experiences, Community & Inspiration
https://www.webdesignerdepot.com/

Dinga, W., Lianga, P., Tangb, A., Vlietc, H. (2014). Knowledge-based approaches in software documentation: A systematic literature review. *Inf. Softw. Technol, 56*(6), 545-567.
[http://dx.doi.org/10.1016/j.infsof.2014.01.008]

Faas, R. (2012). 10 mistakes that can sink an app, a mobile site, and a company's reputation
https://www.cultofmac.com/

Ferre, X., Juristo, N., Windl, H., Constantine, L. (2001). Usability basics for software developers. *IEEE Softw, 18*(1), 22-29.
[http://dx.doi.org/10.1109/52.903160]

Fetaji, M., Dika, Z., Fetaji, B. (2008). Usability testing and evaluation of a mobile software solution: a case study. *30th International Conference on Information Technology Interfaces,* 501-506.
[http://dx.doi.org/10.1109/ITI.2008.4588461]

Grossman, T., Fitzmaurice, G., Attar, R. (2009). A survey of software learnability: Metrics, methodologies and guidelines.*CHI 2009 Metrics*. Boston, Massachusetts, USA: ACM.
[http://dx.doi.org/10.1145/1518701.1518803]

Heimdahl, M., Leveson, N. (1996). Completeness and consistency in hierarchical state-based requirements. *IEEE Trans. Softw. Eng, 22*(6), 363-377.
[http://dx.doi.org/10.1109/32.508311]

Holzinger, A. (2005). Usability engineering methods for software developers. *Commun. ACM, 48*(1), 71-74.
[http://dx.doi.org/10.1145/1039539.1039541]

Software engineering product quality part 1: quality model, 20 Software engineering — Software product Quality Requirements and Evaluation (SQuaRE) — Requirements for quality of Commercial Off-The-Shelf (COTS) software product and instructions for testing.

James, J. (2009). How intuitive should developers make software?, In Software Engineer, in Tech & Work *techrepublic.*

Jonathan, A. (2013). *What accessibility standards apply to mobile applications?*.https://www.levelaccess.com/

Kaptelinin, V. (1993). Item recognition in menu selection: The effect of practice.*Proceedings of Human Factors in Computing Systems (InterCHI 93)* ACM Press.
[http://dx.doi.org/10.1145/259964.260196]

KPMG. (2014). *Addressing mobile applications risk: A software quality focus. Technical report.* KPMG LLP, Swiss.

Kurniawan, S. (2007). Mobile phone design for older persons. *Interactions, ACM, 14*(4), 24-25.
[http://dx.doi.org/10.1145/1273961.1273979]

Lee, B., Bederson, B. (2003). *Favorite folders: A configurable, scalable file browser. tech report hcil-200--12, cs-tr-4468, umiacs-tr-2003-38, Technical report.* College Park, MD: Computer Science Department, University of Maryland.

Leung, R., McGrenere, J., Graf, P. (2008). The learnability of mobile application interfaces needs improvement. *British HCI Workshop on HCI and the Older Population.*

Lian, Y., Shan, L., Yu, S., Shuang, S. (2008). Completeness and consistency analysis on requirements of distributed event-driven systems. *2ⁿᵈ IFIP/IEEE International Symposium on Theoretical Aspects of Software Engineering,* 241-244.

Margaret, R. (2011). interactivity. Technical report *TechTarget.*

McKay, E. (2010). *Intuitive ui: What the heck is it?– User Experience Design Training & Consulting.* UX DESIGN EDGE.

Monge, R., Marco, F., Cervigon, F. (2002). An assessment of the consistency for software measurement methods. *ArXiv Computer Science e-prints,* 1-7.

Nielsen, J. (1993). Usability engineering. In Morgan Kaufmann, Nielsen Norman Group, *World Leaders in Research-Based User Experience, USA Inc., San Francisco, CA.*

Nielsen, J. (2010). ipad usability: First findings from user testing. Nielsen Norman Group *World Leaders in Research-Based User Experience.*

Norman, D. (2010). Natural user interfaces are not natural. *Interactions, ACM, 17*(3), 1-5. [http://dx.doi.org/10.1145/1744161.1744163]

OGCIO. (2018). *Mobile Application Accessibility Handbook.* The Government of the Hong Kong Special Administrative Region.

Patrick, C. (2012). Maintaining consistency in your ui design *designshack.net.*

Payne, A. (2007). *Minimalism in code.* https://al3x.net/posts/2007/11/30/minimalism-in-code.html

Rock, L. (2011). *Improving the learnability of mobile devices for older adults.*

Ronald, G. (1978). *A qualitative justification for a measure of program clarity.*

User control,Imprint German. salfeld.com. (2015).

Sauro, J. (2013). *How to measure learnability.* https://measuringu.com/

Seffah, A., Metzker, E. (2004). The obstacles and myths of usability and software engineering. *Commun. ACM, 47*(12), 71-76. [http://dx.doi.org/10.1145/1035134.1035136]

Skelton, M. (2014). *Operability: A Devops Cornerstone.* Highops.

Spriestersbach, A., Springer, T. (2004). *Quality attributes in mobile web application development. lncs 3009, proceedings of profes, berlin* Springer-Verlag.

Vangie, B. (2015). *API - Application program interface.* Webopedia, QuinStreet Inc.

CHAPTER 4

Charisma: Do Mobile Applications have Charisma?

Abstract: This chapter focuses on the charisma of a mobile application as one of the main qualitative characteristics. The chapter begins with the uniqueness of the mobile application and explores user satisfaction while using the mobile application. This chapter discusses the professionalism displayed by the application and mainly emphasizes the best features of the mobile application that can attract users. It also discusses the curiosity feature and focuses on the entrancement of mobile applications. The chapter considers the hype of mobile applications and discusses the expectancy and attitude of mobile applications.

Keywords: Best Features, Charisma, Curiosity, Entrancement, Expectancy and Attitude of Mobile Applications, Mobile Application, Qualitative Characteristics, Uniqueness of Mobile Application, User Satisfaction.

1. INTRODUCTION

This chapter focuses on the charisma of a mobile application as one of the main qualitative characteristics in a mobile application. This chapter is divided into eleven sections. The chapter begins with an introduction followed by section 4.2 with a pictorial representation of the different subsections that add to the charisma of the mobile application. Section 4.3 discusses the uniqueness of the mobile application and section 4.4 explores user satisfaction while using the mobile application. Section 4.5 discusses the professionalism displayed by the application, and section 4.6 focuses on the best features of the mobile application that attracts users. Section 4.7 discusses the curiosity of the mobile application, and section 4.8 focuses on the entrancement of mobile applications. Section 4.9 considers the hype of mobile applications, whereas sections 4.10 and 4.11 discuss the expectancy and attitude of mobile applications, respectively. Section 4.12 discusses the user's impression. Finally, section 4.13 discusses the story behind developing mobile applications.

Mohamed Sarrab, Hafedh Al-Shihi and Naveen Safia

2. CHARISMA

The new Oxford American Dictionary (Oxford, 2010) defines charisma as a compelling attractiveness or charm that can inspire devotion in others'. While this might be true with humans, mobile applications also have a set of factors that make them worthwhile and, at times, compelling too in the eyes of users. What makes people devote more attention to WhatsApp as opposed to other similar messaging applications? Why do we choose to use one photo-editing app over the other?

Moreover, when searching for new applications in any category, what makes you choose one app over the other?

In this chapter, we explore eleven factors that add charisma to mobile applications (see Fig. **4**). Mobile application developers aim to increase the charm of their applications by incorporating as many attractive features as possible. As we believe the list need not be comprehensive, it records the most vital charismatic elements of a mobile app.

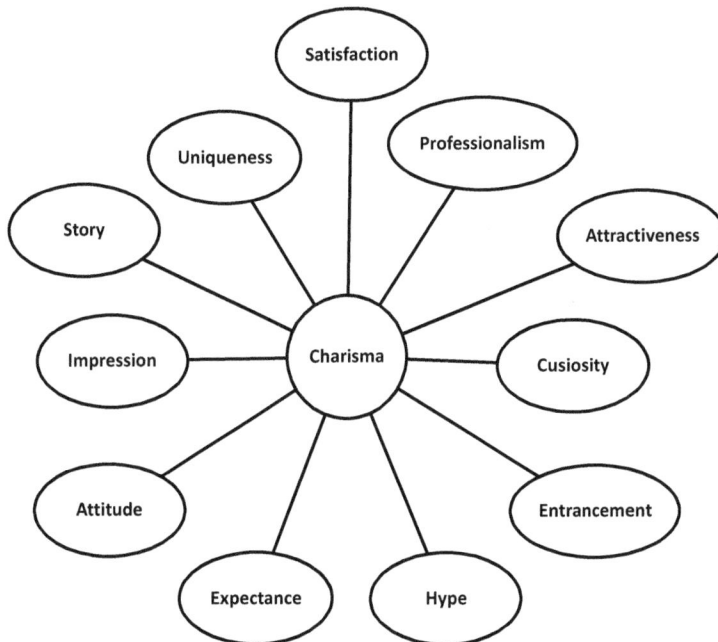

Fig. (4). Mobile Application Charisma Determinants.

Subsequent sections describe each of the eleven mobile application factors that contribute to charisma: uniqueness, satisfaction, professionalism, attractiveness, curiosity, entrancement, hype, expectancy, attitude, directness, and story. Applications in different categories may incorporate different sets of these factors. For example, business and productivity applications may incorporate professionalism more as opposed to apps in the entertainment and game categories where attractiveness is vital.

3. UNIQUENESS

Innovation is the key in mobile applications, and usually, the early adopters of exclusive and distinct features take the lead. In mobile applications, 'uniqueness' refers to how distinguishable the application is from the other applications and whether it offers something that no other application does. This is hard to accomplish as mobile applications become more mature in certain categories. Laggards and latecomers in mobile application development tend to follow leaders in the field. After all, this is what is benchmarking as a management tool suggests. See for example how the messaging application 'Telegram' tried to distinguish itself from the ubiquitous 'WhatsApp' by adding killer features such as increasing the number of users in chat groups (currently 100 users in WhatsApp and 200 in Telegram) in addition to waiving file size restrictions when sharing media files (16 MB restriction in WhatsApp).

Unfortunately, 'uniqueness' does not mean exclusiveness, as mobile developers tend to imitate what users like in other apps more often than innovating new features. This has forced several companies to file lawsuits against each other in an attempt to protect their intellectual properties and/or discourage developers from following them. The well-known battle in the court of law between Apple and Samsung is a very good example here. Nevertheless, developers must continuously strive to offer unique features to stay competitive, as 'uniqueness' tends to fade out over time. That is why 'WhatsApp' had to introduce voice calling lately in response to users' demands and the proliferation of messaging apps with the same feature (Shafriri and Levy, 2018).

4. SATISFACTION

What makes users use one mobile application over another in the same category? Why 'Evernote' is more popular than so many other note-taking applications? Why do we choose to download a different web browser or email client when all mobile devices come with stock mobile browsers and emails? Users tend to like, get used to, and are more satisfied with certain mobile apps than others. This leads to the question, what shapes this satisfaction?

The concept of 'satisfaction' is used in marketing, management, and computer science to determine people's attitudes towards a specific goal. In marketing, the focus is usually on customers' satisfaction with the products/services, whereas in management; job satisfaction is more vital (Ang and Koh, 1997). On the other hand, computer science likes to measure users' satisfaction with the computer system/program interface, operations, and produced outputs. In all cases, 'satisfaction' is usually linked with expectations and features required. As a result, we may define it as how a certain mobile app meets users' expectations and needs. The opposite, in this case, will be 'frustration', which is a state of feeling caused by dissatisfaction or disapproval of the overall mobile application experience.

It is crucial here to pinpoint that satisfaction is an overall feeling of the whole experience with the mobile application. This feeling is highly influenced by expectations. Users in general download mobile applications to fulfill a specific need about which they have built a certain level of expectations. Whether the downloaded app meets users' expectations partially or fully, determines their level of satisfaction and continued use of the app or not. It is worth noting that we have mentioned users' expectations, but not requirements. Managing expectations always emphasizes the difference between the two terms. Expectations are usually shaped by users' previous experiences, whereas requirements are related to its feature. In satisfaction, the emphasis is on meeting and managing users' expectations. You will learn in the next section that requirements are crucial to determine the professionalism of the application. Therefore, mobile developers are advised to ensure users' satisfaction by understanding and managing their expectations about the requirements (Bailey and Pearson, 1983).

5. PROFESSIONALISM

People choose to browse apps in a specific category based upon their needs. Each category comes with a different set of aims. For example, apps in the health and fitness category have a different list of requirements from that of business and education. We expect health and fitness apps to be able to provide health-related measurements and/or advise on our fitness routine. We do not expect or need health apps to provide us with notes and photo-taking functions, although they could be integrated with other related functions. For example, Mobile Smith Hospital Apps (MobileSmith, 2015) have incorporated these features to allow doctors to communicate with patients and prescribe medicines at the same time. Nevertheless, there is a minimum list of requirements in each mobile app category where developers try to embrace and build upon.

'Professionalism' is defined by (Merriam-Webster, 2015) as the conduct, aims, or qualities that characterize a profession or a professional. The same principles can also be applied to mobile apps to ensure they do exactly what they are supposed to. A professional app is supposed to meet its purpose not only in terms of functions but also in terms of the look and feel preferences of the target users. For a mobile app to have a professional flair and feel, it should accurately meet the needs and requirements of its primary category and tailor it to the target audience. A drawing app for kids may share some basic drawing requirements with a similar app for professional artists; however, both should be customized to offer a different experience to their intended audience. Kids enjoy simpler and amusing features supported by multimedia walkthrough clips. Artists, on the other hand, appreciate intuitive designs, fluid processing speed, and advanced drawing tools. This is usually achieved in the app interface design and the agreed list of features.

6. ATTRACTIVENESS

Mobile app development is not always about introducing distinct features. Elements like usability, design, accessibility become vital to ensure wider users. Moreover, the choice of themes, colors, fonts, animation, and multimedia are essential too. Developers must aim to find the perfect balance and match between these elements to make their applications more attractive. Attractiveness in a mobile app device refers to how appealing the application to users' eyes and all other senses. The focus should be on making apps look and feel easy, smooth, comfortable, and pleasing to users as much as possible. It should incorporate a 'WOW' user experience at the inception (which is discussed in more detail later under the title 'Impression') and retain the feeling throughout its use.

Unfortunately, attractiveness is not always within developers' control since it is highly affected by the hardware of the device. Mobile manufacturers build devices with different screens and specs. The latest and the most advanced display resolution, for example, is Quad Ultra High Definition (QUHD) with a 15360x8640 pixels resolution although it is not yet available for mobiles.

Recently, mobile devices started getting 4k displays, which support a 4096x2160 pixels resolution. Screen technologies vary as well and each has its benefits and drawbacks. For example, Active-Matrix Organic Light Emitting Diode (AMOLED) displays are perfect for color reproduction with very deep black and offer great viewing angles, but are more expensive to produce and suffer sharpness when looking up close. Liquid Crystal Displays (LCD) on the other hand comes in different types, all of which are much brighter than AMOLED and produce more accurate and realistic colors. Mobile app developers may recommend their apps to be installed on devices with certain hardware specs but usually, they keep it to a minimum to cater to a wider audience (Anurag, 2019).

7. CURIOSITY

The proliferation of mobile apps in iOS, Android, and Windows platforms poses a huge pressure on developers to find ways to stand out. While marketing strategies may help in spreading awareness, they should aim also to establish an interest and/or curiosity in users to try out mobile applications. In this sense, curiosity refers to a state of feeling or a desire to explore, investigate, and/or learn about a certain app. It should be considered as a lesser level of interest and is usually not related to an urgent or genuine need or requirement. Users opt to test an app only if it fulfills a real need (interest), or it has sparked a probing feeling (curiosity) and have time for it.

Marketing tools could certainly help in establishing curiosity but sometimes it is hard to justify or meet its cost. With today's advancements in IT and web 2.0 applications, there are numerous ways to promote curiosity without spending a dime. Word of mouth is an effective marketing tool, which can be tapped through social media, along with app reviewers' websites. Blogging, YouTube, and podcasts also certainly help. Press publicity, forums, teaser videos, and how-t--series may as well collaboratively create curiosity in customers.

8. ENTRANCEMENT

This factor deals with the immersive experience that users receive in the application. We define entrancement as the users' level of engagement and immersion with a mobile app. This factor is associated more with applications in the entertainment, social networking, and gaming category. The idea is to provide the user with a hooked experience through an interesting and amusing flow of operations/activities. Apps in other categories may have some 'entrancement' (immersive) feeling in fields such as in news and education, production, and photo and video, but are restricted to content and/or features.

Entrancement if properly planned and incorporated into the app workflow design, may trigger a craving for the product and loyalty. This influences users' acceptance and eventually their buying decisions, which fuel higher profitability. Users may experience higher levels of entrancement in different genres of games. Minecraft, a game set in a virtual world where players must survive by building a shelter is a good example of how entrancement can come into play. In a short time, it helped to create tens of millions of players in a competitive and addicting phenomenon (Ward, 2013).

9. HYPE

Mobile technologies evolve rapidly both in software and hardware. Popular mobile platforms such as iOS from Apple and Android from Google are cycled for an annual update which usually introduces new features and tools. For example, Apple has recently introduced a 3D touch feature (recognizing the different levels of screen pressure) across the new iPhone 6s and 6s+ where mobile developers are yet to consider and embrace. Android's latest version code, named 'marshmallow' supports USB Type-C, a reversible USB plug that is faster in charging and data sharing. Mobile manufacturers are also innovating new tools and features and encouraging developers to exploit the latest in their apps.

Such technological advancements and users' growing demands to use the latest mobile tools pose pressure on mobile developers to adopt. Mobile apps with a 'hype' factor are those with support to the latest technologies. 'Hype' in this sense is the application of state-of-the-art technology tools and features, early on, to get the advantage of craving users. Every year, Apple highlights its new technologies by inviting selected early adopters to present their offers on stage during Apple special events. This provides a great level of 'hype' to the participating developers and their apps.

10. EXPECTANCY

Expectations of the users were discussed earlier in the 'Satisfaction' feature where the importance of meeting the overall expectations of the users to ensure app satisfaction is emphasized. However, developers also consider those features, which the app exceeds or aims to exceed users' expectations? "Under promise, over-perform" is an old controversial adage, which suggests that apps should always meet the expectations of people at the least while aiming to deliver higher results. In other words, apps should attempt to exceed the expectations of the user and aim to alleviate app 'expectancy'. In this sense, we define 'expectancy' as the degree to which an app meets the expectations of the user about the available and required features, as opposed to 'satisfaction' where the focus is on the overall experience.

While meeting the expectations of users is the key to satisfaction, it may cause it to be more predictable, and less attractive and appealing to users especially when it focuses only on the included features. Developers should study the expectations of the users along with the current state of play in related app categories to define a framework for design and implementation that surpasses their hopes and needs. Offering users more innovative features than expected is sure to create a welcoming 'WOW' factor and a great value for their money. This could be achieved not only by introducing new features and tools but also by re-engineering outdated operations and simplifying tasks and activities.

11. ATTITUDE

Attitude is defined in psychology as a positive or negative evaluation of something such as people, objects, events, activities, and ideas (Allport, 1935). Positivity and negativity in humans are determined by social influences, which usually affect the individual's desire to change his/her beliefs and behaviors McGuire (1985). Psychologists claim that a positive attitude highly correlates with good relationships, better health, and a higher rate of success in life. In this respect, people always prefer to surround themselves with positive people.

Extending the same philosophy to mobile computing, an app's 'attitude' refers to the methodology or approach, which ensures consistency in the continuous interaction and usage of the users. In other words, does the app take care of its users? Apps with positive attitudes are those which regularly provide app updates to users to enhance services and tools. Some of them are security issues (Sarrab and Alnaeli, 2018), fixing bugs, customizing and localizing experiences of the user, preserving the privacy of the users (Alkindi *et al.*, 2019), and maintaining solid quality measures. On the other hand, a negative 'attitude' is associated with apps that provide inconsistent experiences and generic services or tools. They are also money-oriented and respond slowly to bugs and complaints.

12. IMPRESSION

A first impression is a mental image made when a person experiences something or someone for the first time (Smith and Mackie, 2007). Mobile users also form first impressions about mobile apps. While humans may take one-tenth of a second to make an impression about other people (Willis and Todorov, 2014), developers usually offer reviewers one to three days to test an app before making their evaluations. As for normal users, they may decide to abandon or like an app soon after its first launch, which varies from few seconds to a few hours of use.

Accordingly, impressions can be defined as an emotional image created by users about a certain mobile app during the first few hours of use. Impressions made about an app may differ based upon the expectations and background of the users. Tech-savvy users are usually hard to impress, just as the long-time users of certain apps or mobile platforms. Developers are advised as always to create a 'WOW' impression which is a combination of 'attractiveness', 'professionalism', 'hype', and lower 'expectancy'. This could be achieved by properly studying target users' preferences against the current state of play to find a niche and innovative features.

13. STORY

The power of word-of-mouth has been discussed in the earlier section about 'curiosity' and the tools that developers may use to promote curiosity in users. Social media and web 2.0 applications are playing a greater role nowadays to build glamorous images of mobile applications. There is always a story behind popular applications, which help to spread awareness and promote higher adoption rates. People and scholars like to use and spread these stories mostly as a sign of success or failure. See for example how the self-destructing photo and video messaging feature in Snapchat motivated millions of people to install the app (Gallagher, 2012). Likewise, 'Instagram' and 'WhatsApp' multi-billion dollar sales deals encouraged millions of users to install and/or remain loyal.

We define 'story' here as a list of thought-provoking events or features associated with one or more milestones in the app life cycle. As stories are memorable, any events and/or features may have happened before or during the development, at the launch of the app, or after maturity, they are used to tell stories to the users. Developers and app owners must utilize interesting events to build and publicize exciting stories about their apps to draw adoption, interest, and curiosity.

SUMMARY

This chapter has focused on the charisma of mobile applications as one of the main quality characteristics. This chapter is divided into twelve sections. Section 4.1 has the introduction and section 4.2 has the pictorial representation of the subsections of charisma. Section 4.3 has discussed the uniqueness of the mobile application while section 4.4 has explored the amount of satisfaction a mobile application provides to its users. This is followed by section 4.5 discussed the professionalism of the application in the way it looks and the way it feels. Section 4.6 has mainly focused on the best way that mobile applications can attract users. Section 4.7 has discussed the curiosity of mobile applications to appeal to a larger group of the audience including those who have used it much and section 4.8 is focused on the entrancement of the mobile application. Section 4.9 has considered the hype of mobile applications which is also important to maintain. Sections 4.10 and 4.11 have discussed the expectancy and attitudes of mobile applications respectively. Section 4.12 discussed the users' impressions. Finally, section 4.13 has discussed the story behind the developing mobile application, which is interesting and memorable to the users as well as potential users.

We are witnessing a proliferation of mobile apps, exceeding a million barriers in iOS and Android. Mobile app developers and owners are struggling to gain a stand in such a mature, fast-evolving, and competitive market. It is therefore crucial for a mobile app to have the flavor of 'charisma'. This chapter has discussed twelve determinants that shape charisma mobile apps. At this stage, we should realize that the list is neither comprehensive nor compulsory. Developers must aim to embrace as many factors as possible bearing in mind the category of the app as well as the target audience. There are obvious overlaps between factors, which we highlighted earlier. While some factors at first may appear relevant to few categories, they may still benefit by expanding their services and embedding new innovative features while maintaining a unique focus.

REFERENCES

Alkindi, Z., Sarrab, M., Alzidi, N. (2019). Android Application Permission Model Issues and Privacy Violation *4th Free and Open Source Software Conference (FOSSC2019)*.Muscat, Oman

Allport, G. (1935). Handbook of Social Psychology, chapter Attitudes, Ang, J., & Koh, S. (1997). Exploring the relationships between user information satisfaction and job satisfaction. *Int. J. Inf. Manage, 17*(3), 169-177.

Anurag, A. (2019). What makes your app attractive to investors https://www.newgenapps.com/

Bailey, J., Pearson, S. (1983). Development of a tool for measuring and analysing computer user satisfaction. *Manage. Sci, 29*(5), 530-545.
[http://dx.doi.org/10.1287/mnsc.29.5.530]

Gallagher, B. (2012). *You know what's cool? a billion snapchats: App sees over 20 million photos shared per day, Technical report, Releases On Android.* TechCrunch.

McGuire, W., Lindzey, G., Aronson, E. (1985). *Attitudes and attitude change. Handbook of social psychology: Special fields and applications.*

Merriam-Webster Professionalism. (2015).

MobileSmith. (2015). *Hospital apps, Apps and Wearables in Healthcare: What Works? A Comprehensive Guide for Healthcare Executives* Clark University Press.

Sarrab, M., Alnaeli, S. (2018). Critical Aspects Pertaining Security of IoT Application Level Software Systems, IEEE IEMCON 2018, 9th IEEE Annul Information Technology *Electronics and Mobile Communication Conference Vancouver Canada.*

Shafriri, Y., Levy, D. (2018). Uniqueness Profile of Mobile Applications for Learning.*Learning and Collaboration Technologies. Learning and Teaching. LCT 2018* Lecture Notes in Computer Science(Vol. 10925). Cham: Springer.
[http://dx.doi.org/10.1007/978-3-319-91152-6_29]

Smith, E., Mackei, D. (2007). *Social psychology* (3rd ed.). Hove: Psychology Press.

Ward, M. (2013). *Why minecraft if more than just another video game, Technology correspondent.* BBC News.

Willis, A., Todorov, J. (2014). First impressions: Making up your mind after 100 ms exposure to a face (pdf). *Psychol. Sci, 17592598*

CHAPTER 5

Security: Does Mobile Application Protect Against Unwanted Usage?

Abstract: This chapter focuses on the security of a mobile application as one of the main qualitative characteristics. The chapter emphasizes the authentication process in the mobile application and explores the authorization mechanism used for a mobile application. It also discusses the users' and applications' information privacy and mainly focuses on mobile application security holes. Finally, it discusses the potential risks of how the personal information of users is treated.

Keywords: Application Information Privacy, Application Security Holes, Authorization Mechanisms, Authentication Process, Mobile Application, Potential Risks, Qualitative Characteristics, Secrecy, Security, User Privacy.

1. INTRODUCTION

This chapter focuses on the security of a mobile application as one of the main qualitative characteristics. This chapter is divided into five sections. The chapter begins with an introduction to the chapter followed by section 5.2 with a pictorial representation of the different subsections that add to the security of the mobile application. Section 5.3 discusses the authentication process in the mobile application and section 5.4 explores the authorization mechanism using a mobile application. Section 5.5 discusses the users' and applications' information privacy and section 5.6 mainly focuses on the mobile application security holes. Finally, section 5.7 discusses the potential risks of the way in which the personal information of users is treated.

2. SECURITY

Security in the mobile application is the enforcement of access, use, and data protection measures for a separate application. Examples of such applications in security regulations and policies include corporate authentication, data wipe, data encryption, app-level VPN, and copy/paste protection. Security policies and regulations can be applied in the application development process, later after the application is compiled with app wrapping or with software development kits (SDKs). Mobile malware usually taps weaknesses and bugs in the development of mobile applications and they attack. Even before exploitation of vulnerability to bugs, attackers can gain a public copy of an application and reverse engineer it (Al-Emran, 2020).

Mobile application developers should be skilled in detecting, fixing, and blocking security vulnerabilities to provide solid applications against tampering and reverse engineering. However, mobile application consumers still represent an application development, as it may not undergo a solid and appropriate security check process. Fig. (**5**) illustrates the mobile application security factors.

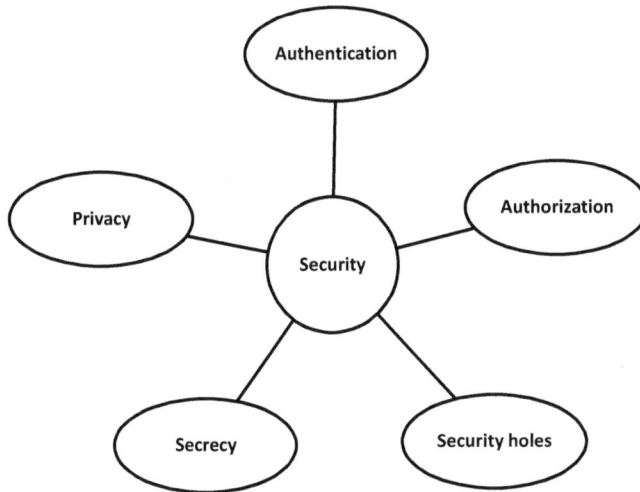

Fig. (5). Mobile Application Security Factors.

Authentication of the mobile application is the identification of users to access and use the application, but the authorization is the permission given to authenticated mobile application users about what they can see and do. Privacy in a mobile application is referred to as the capability to protect data and not disclose this data to unauthorized users of the application.

Security holes in a mobile application are related to the detection and closing of social engineering vulnerabilities. The secrecy of mobile applications is to prevent disclosing any type of information about the underlying systems under any circumstances. Invulnerability is the ability of the application to withstand penetration efforts. Mobile applications should be free of viruses as they will not transport or appear as a virus. Mobile applications should be compliant with different security standards.

3. AUTHENTICATION

The most essential requirement to build a mobile application that is fully secure is to have a solution to authenticate users for an application. The authentication process in mobile applications verifies whether application users are those who they claim to be, using their identity and credentials (for example, username and password). User identification of mobile applications is a logical entity used to identify mobile application users. User identification is used to distinguish between different users who attempt to access or use the mobile application. User identification is one of the most popular authentication mechanisms that is utilized within different computing applications. Irrespective of the user types and rights, every mobile application user has a unique ID (identification) that distinguishes users from other mobile application users. Usually, in an authentication mechanism, the user ID is used in conjunction with a password. The mobile application end-user has to provide both the credentials (ID and password) correctly to gain access to the application. Moreover, administrators can track user activity, assign user rights, and manage overall operations on a particular mobile application (Ulrike, 2014).

Today many breaches are found in mobile applications because of weak authentication mechanisms, from cracked passwords to unlocked mobile devices. In some cases, there is no authentication mechanism at all. Many awkward and expensive incidents could be avoided with the use of a robust authentication mechanism to access mobile applications. Planning a strategy for authentication of mobile applications needs to consider enforceability and strength with usability. That should be able to satisfy security and user requirements. It is common to use the password for the authentication mechanism to authenticate users of the mobile application. But we also know that generally, mobile application access passwords might be easily guessed. Thus users should be forced to have rules regarding complexity, length, and timeout. If a wrong password is used, the phone becomes inactive for a while. Saving the user name and password on the phone should also be discouraged. With these measures, it is possible to make the mobile application very hard to access by anyone other than the users.

Some mobile applications support a two-step verification mechanism using the application itself. For example, a mobile application for twitter permits users to enable login verification. Whenever user endeavors to log into the Twitter application from another device, where the user has to verify that login attempt from the mobile application on a phone device. Twitter inspects to guarantee the user has access to the phone before he/ she attempts to log in. Apple has a two-step verification mechanism that works similar to Twitter, even though it does not use an application (application level) it uses iOS itself (operating system level). Whenever user endeavors to log in from another device, a one-time-use code is received by the user that is sent to the registered new device, such as iPad or iPhone (Dobeomir, 2007).

4. AUTHORIZATION

User authorization of mobile application is granting or denying access to that application. Most mobile security systems use a two-step process. The first step is the authentication step where the user is identified. It ensures that the application user is the one who he claims to be. The second step is the authorization step, which is about allowing the user to access an application after checking the user's identity. An authorization process is giving users permission to have or do something such as type of access to which files, directories, amount of allocated storage space, hours of access ... *etc.*

An application administrator can define the access and privilege rights of application users. In case a mobile application user has logged into an application, then the application can identify what resources a user can access and manipulate during this session. Accordingly, the authorization process can be seen as a preliminary set of permissions by an application administrator and an inspection of the permission value that has been set up when the application user is granted access (Margaret, 2014).

A mobile application user must gain application authorization to perform certain tasks. For example, after logging into an application, the application user may try to perform commands. Then the application authorization process checks and controls whether the current user has the authority to perform such commands. Authorization is a mechanism

- to enforce policies and regulations;
- determine what types of activities, services, and resources is permitted to an application user and
- determine control mechanisms.

Generally, authorization of mobile applications takes place within the context of authentication. When users are authenticated, they can be authorized for different types of access, resource, or activity at the same time (Dag-Inge, 2013).

The authorization process should be exercised whenever there is a need to control access and rights of certain pages, for example, the E-learning system in Sultan

Qaboos University can be accessed through mobile devices. But not all students are authorized to access certain web pages that are dedicated to different courses, professors, and administration. Authentication and Authorization processes are regularly used together. For example, students at Sultan Qaboos University are asked to authenticate before accessing their portal. Their authentication process determines what information they are authorized to view and manipulate and the user authorization process prevents them from viewing and manipulating other students' information.

However, in some cases, there is no need for an authorization process to take place and the users may access a file or use a resource directly without any barriers. Authentication or authorization are not required in most web pages that are available on the Internet. For example, accessing the Sultan Qaboos university web page does not require any type of authentication or authorization for the students, staff, administrators, and guests (Akinyemi, 2002), (Nauman and Al-Khanjari, 2011).

5. PRIVACY

A typical mobile system consists of several different components, including the device, used operating systems, and the application itself. The mobile environment has specific features that are personal to the user. Therefore the main concern is the privacy of an application (Sarrab and Alshohoumi, 2019). Privacy in a mobile application is defined as an individual's right to be free from interference or intrusion by others. It refers to the ability of an individual or group to isolate or seclude themselves, or any information about them, and thus can express themselves as needed or as selectively. Mobile application users have different privacy interests concerning their used application type, personal information, and user communications with others and share resources as needed (Sarrab and Bourdoucen, 2013), (Sarrab and Alshohoumi, 2020).

The boundaries and restrictions on the content that is considered private differ from user to user though they share common themes. Once something is considered private to a mobile application user, it means that this content is sensitive or inherently special to the user (Alkindi *et al.*, 2020). An important aspect of privacy in a mobile application is the user's right to control the information about himself/ herself and the application that he uses. In reality, the field of privacy in mobile applications partially overlaps with security, especially confidentiality as confidentiality can include the concepts of protection and control of information as well as appropriate use of that information. Mobile application privacy may also be considered as a form of mobile application integrity (Sarrab and Elbasir, 2015), (AlAbdali *et al.*, 2019).

To maintain the privacy of mobile application users, the developers must consider forming a privacy policy regarding 3 issues: to describe the data manipulation, the way it can be used, and the way it can be shared. Users need to know how and where data will flow throughout an application execution, and how these data/information will be controlled during the life cycle of the mobile application. The application developer should understand all application perspectives and then communicate the same to application users and should not fail to disclose material information or miss a statement about the practical use of data which is disclosed in the applicable privacy policy (UK-ICO, 2013), (USA-FTC, 2013), (Alkindi, 2020).

6. SECURITY HOLES

Social engineering has gained growing acceptance in the mobile application community as an effective social method for exploiting the mobile application security mechanism. Social engineering remains a popular technique of compromising the security of social engineering vulnerabilities in mobile applications. Phishing is related to malicious parties that send a fraudulent email, received as a legitimate email, often claiming to be sent from a trusted source. The email contents always seek to gain the recipient's personal or financial information or provide a link that needs to be clicked to install malware. Spear phishing is similar to normal phishing but tailored for a particular individual (Bakhshi and Papadaki, 2008), (Margaret, 2016).

Different factors contribute to vulnerabilities in mobile applications such as side loading, malware, bad data storage practices, and lack of encryption. The users of mobile applications need to understand the best practices for granting permissions and downloading an application. Vulnerabilities of Android mobile applications have become an issue because of the open format of Google Market, as well as the users' ability to side load apps; whereas users can install applications on a mobile device without using the official platform method of application distribution such as Apple Store or Google Play. Google Play is still not fully protected from malware attacks. The developers of malicious mobile applications break up malware into pieces to avoid detection and they use the popular applications' names to entice for downloading the malware.

Inexperienced mobile application programmers are the main reason for the existence of vulnerabilities in the mobile application as they usually have bad data storage habits. Databases such as SQLite make it easy to store compact data on a local device, but an inexperienced programmer usually stores data in a readable XML format or clear text. It is easy to gain access to an application's data through a plain-text file. Such vulnerabilities force users to encrypt sensitive data at the device level, as well as encrypt external connections. Mobile applications that do not use encryption can cause many issues as well. The developers of mobile applications should use common encryption frameworks to protect users' information (Heary, 2010), (Margaret, 2016).

The best way to protect mobile applications against malware and other vulnerabilities is to teach users about access permissions after an application is installed. Moreover, security specialists recommend a mobile application to regularly go through penetration tests that use different social engineering techniques.

7. SECRECY

The mobile application environment presents different potential risks of how the personal information of users is treated. Usually, the correctness of mobile applications is verified and performance is evaluated based on security properties such as confidentiality, integrity, and availability. The more secret and sensitive the information being processed by a mobile application, the more essential it is to ensure the secrecy and privacy of this information such as personal medical information, banking information, or personal emails or messages. The processed information during mobile application execution should be monitored and controlled to prevent any leaks of information to any channel that is not trusted. To maintain secrecy, the developed mobile application should consider the interaction with the user.

In case a violation occurs, the user should be presented with an understandable chain of flow that enables the mobile user to decide whether to grant the flow, create an exception, or terminate the application program (Australian-OAIC, 2014), (USA-FTC, 2013).

In general, the mobile application would be users' ally in supporting users to protect their private information, which they do not want to propagate. Most of the time, mobile application users have information that is secretive and should not be disseminated to the public. This does not mean that there is anything illegal or bad. It is information like secret files, Internet Protocol (IP) addresses, pictures, emails, messages, contact lists, Unique Device Identifiers (UDIDs), location information, and other unique identifiers in specific circumstances ... *etc.* Thus the developed mobile application would put an end to the users' privacy invasion. Moreover, under any circumstance, the mobile application should not disclose information about the underlying systems. The mobile application developers are required to take reasonable steps to protect users' personal information from any loss, interference, or misuse as well as disclosure, modification, and even unauthorized access (Imai and Zheng, 2000), (Sarrab and Bourdoucen, 2013).

SUMMARY

This chapter has discussed the security of a mobile application as one of its main qualitative attributes. It has introduced the security of mobile applications. This chapter has been divided into five sections, where each section describes a different sub-quality characteristic. Section 5.3 has discussed the users' authentication process and section 5.4 has explored the authorization mechanism using the mobile application. Section 5.5 has discussed users' and applications' information privacy, and section 5.6 has focused on the mobile application security holes. Finally, section 5.7 discussed the potential risks of how the personal information of users is treated.

REFERENCES

Ahmad, N., Al-Khanjari, Z. (2011). Effect of moodle on learning: An oman perception. *International Journal of Digital Information and Wireless Communications,* *1*(4), 746-752. [IJDIWC].

Akinyemi, A. (2002). E-learn: World conference on e-learning in corporate, government, healthcare, and higher education. In World Conferene of E-Learn, ISBN 978-1-880094-46-4, Montreal, Canada *Association for the Advancement of Computing in Education (AACE), Chesapeake, VA.*

AlAbdali, H., Al-Badawi, M., Sarrab, M. (2019). Preserving Privacy of Integrated E-Government Information: Architecture Approach, *the 2019 IEEE Middle East & North Africa COMMunications Conference (MENACOMM 2019), Manama, Kingdom of Bahrain.*

Al-Emran, M., Granić, A., Al-Sharafi, M., Ameen, N., Sarrab, M. (2020). Examining the roles of students' beliefs and security concerns for using smartwatches in higher education *Journal of Enterprise Information Management, Emerald Publishing Limited.*

Alkindi, Z., Sarrab, M., Alzidi, N. (2020). CUPA : A Configurable User Privacy Approach for Android Mobile Application *IEEE International Conference on Edge Computing and Scalable Cloud (IEEE EdgeCom).*

Alkindi, Z., Sarrab, M., Alzidi, N. (2020). CUPA : A Configurable User Privacy Approach for Android Mobile Application *IEEE International Conference on Edge Computing and Scalable Cloud (IEEE EdgeCom).*

Australian-OAIC. (2014). *Mobile privacy a better practice guide for mobile app developers.* https://www.oaic.gov.au/privacy/guidance-and-advice/mobile-privacy-a-better-practice-g-ide-for-mobile-app-develo pers/

Bakhshi, T., Papadaki, M. (2008). *Social engineering vulnerabilities, section 1 network systems engineering.* Technical report, Centre for Information Security and Network Research, University of Plymouth, Plymouth, United Kingdom.

Dag-Inge, A. (2013). Authentication and authorization for native mobile applications using oauth2.0, Master's thesis, Norwegian University of Science and Technology.

Dobeomir, T. (2007). *Mechanics of User Identi?cation and Authentication, Fundamentals of Identity Management.* Auerbach Publication, Taylor & Francis Group NeW York.

Heary, J. (2009). *Network world, top 5 social engineering exploit techniques.* https://www.pcworld.com/article/182180/top_5_social_engineering_exploit_techniques.html

Imai, H., Zheng, Y. (2000). Forward secrecy and its application to future mobile communications security. LNCS. *Springer-Verlag Berlin Heidelberg, 1751*, 433.

Margaret, R. (2014). Authorization, Essential Guide:Develop an IAM strategy for the mobile enterprise http://searchsoftwarequality.techtarget.com/definition/authorization

Sarrab, M., Alshohoumi, F. (2016). Social engineering. Essential Guide: How to hone an effective vulnerability management program Technical report *Tech Target.*

Sarrab, M., Alshohoumi, F. (2020). Privacy Concerns in IoT a Deeper Insight into Privacy Concerns in IoT Based Healthcare. *International Journal of Computing and Digital Systems, 9*(3), 399-418. [http://dx.doi.org/10.12785/ijcds/090306]

Sarrab, M., Bourdoucen, H. (2013). Runtime monitoring using policy based approach to control information flow for mobile apps. *International Journal of Communication Science and Engineering, 7*(11), 913-920.

Sarrab, M., Elbasir, M. (2015). Mobile application: Information flow control. Almadar Journal for Communications. *Information Technology and Applications, 2*(1), 2-11. [AJCITA].

UK-ICO. (2013). UK-ICO. (2013). Team. Privacy in mobile apps guidance for app developers. Technical report, Information Commissioner Office (ICO), UK, V!, https://ico.org.uk/media/for-organisations/documents/1596/privacy-in-mobile-apps-dp-guidance.pdf

Ulrike, S. (2014). Human-Computer Interaction. Applications and Services, volume 8512, chapter Identification of User Requirements for Mobile Applications to Support Door-to-Door Mobility in Public Transport. *Lect. Notes Comput. Sci, 513-524.

USA-FTC. (2013). *Mobile privacy disclosures, building trust through transparency.* https://www.ftc.gov/sites/default/files/documents/reports/mobile-privacy-disclosures-building-trust -throug- -transparency-federal-trade-commission-staff-report/130201mobileprivacyreport.pdf

CHAPTER 6

Performance: Is the Mobile Application Fast Enough?

Abstract: This chapter discusses performance as one of the main qualitative characteristics of a mobile application. It focuses on the limitations of mobile applications in different circumstances. This chapter explores appropriate usage of memory and storage and emphasizes the speed of performing any task or action. It discusses the application availability when needed and mainly focuses on the ability of the application to process many tasks. Besides, it explores how the application can deal with the long-time loading and focuses on the appropriateness of application feedback. Finally, this chapter explores how an application can scale up, scale down, or scale-out.

Keywords: Application Feedback, Availability, Long Time Loading, Mobile Application, Performance, Qualitative Characteristics, Speed of Performing, Usage of Memory and Storage.

1. INTRODUCTION

This chapter focuses on performance as one of the main qualitative characteristics of a mobile application. The chapter is divided into ten sections, where section 6.1 is the introduction and section 6.2 is a pictorial representation of all the subsections of the chapter. Section 6.3 discusses the limitations of mobile applications in different circumstances. Section 6.4 explores the appropriate usage of memory and storage. Section 6.5 discusses the speed of performing any task or action. Section 6.6 discusses application availability when needed. Section 6.7 mainly focuses on the ability of the application to process many tasks. Section 6.8 explores how the application can deal with the long-time loading, and section 6.9 focuses on the appropriateness of application feedback. Section 6.10 discusses how an application can scale up, scale down, or scale-out.

2. PERFORMANCE

Generally, performance is about the user's perception of the appropriateness of the

Mohamed Sarrab, Hafedh Al-Shihi and Naveen Safia

application's performance. The application's performance is measured by its responsiveness and how quickly it starts up the process, and how well an application consumes the device memory and power. In a mobile application, performance can be measured through different factors, including capacity, resource utilization, responsiveness, availability, throughput, endurance, feedback, and scalability (see Fig. **6**).

Fig. (6). Mobile Application Performance Factors.

3. CAPACITY

Capacity has always been crucial to the success of mobile technology in general and mobile learning in particular. Even if there are small improvements in the capacity of mobile applications and technology, it leads to better performance and more user satisfaction. Mobile technology provides users the same access level anytime and anywhere *via* mobile devices with more benefits in terms of increased functions to allow users to engage and interact with mobile applications in novel and compelling ways.

Developing a successful mobile application requires a rigorous analysis of the available technological infrastructure and capacity. It also requires proper planning and considering the demands of the new program, which include software, hardware, technical support, and broadband access.

Developers of mobile applications should consider some important factors such as the capacity which is required to install the application on different mobile devices. Due to the limitations of computational power and memory capacity in mobile devices, the developers have to remove or modify some of the functions such as high image resolution or many windows of the user interface to ensure the usability of the designed mobile application. The wireless connectivity should be available and reliable throughout a study campus to get the maximum benefit. The increase in the usage of a mobile application requires extra data storage capacity.

Improved mobile infrastructure is very important to achieve the full advantage offered by the technological revolution. Better capacity for the wireless network is required for users to improve mobile accessibility level and get the benefit of the available multi-media resources that are offered online. This involves simplifying and creating faster mobile networks. Therefore, the mobile application developer should think about the future connectives through wireless networks. As wifi connection alone cannot support the broadband demand of heavy multimedia resources (AppDynamics, 2015).

4. RESOURCE UTILIZATION

Each mobile application consists of different resources for mobile devices. Device memory and storage utilization of mobile devices are effective factors of performance in a mobile application. The base resources such as battery, CPU, and memory can influence each other; for example, CPU performance speed affects memory usage and CPU utilization affects battery consumption (Rawassizadeh, 2009).

In designing a mobile application, it is essential to consider different constraints of the target device resource including appropriate use of storage and memory. Every decision in designing should take into consideration of the limited memory and storage capacity of the target device. The processor's speed of the device and reading from memory and writing from memory all have an impact on the overall application's performance.

Memory and storage utilization on a mobile device is constrained by its hardware capability and unreliable network connections. For the best memory and storage utilization, the developers must consider three factors: the effect of high latency, intermittent connectivity, and low bandwidth on the overall application design. The impact of performance in an application can be minimized by designing efficient memory, storage access and always using a data reader when reading and not writing data. Moreover, the developer should consider programming an application for data integrity. Any data files that remain open while the power of the device fails or execution is suspended, may cause data integrity issues (MSDN, 2016).

Consequently, it is necessary to keep in mind the shortage of resources in terms of memory and storage. Therefore, in optimizing the developed application, the memory footprint should be minimized.

5. RESPONSIVENESS

The users of mobile applications usually define performance as how well the application performs. This means the performance is measured based on its response. It uses its memory and power in the startup in a way where images, animations, or games behave smoothly. Mobile application users' expectation of responsiveness depends on the type of operating system/device they use. It is clear when we consider how users utilize their phones and how they utilize their web browser, which is not the same.

One significant difference between desktop and mobile applications is the need to tailor the application for the several capabilities and characteristics of a specific mobile device. A mobile application can be designed and optimized to provide a mobile-appropriate experience and mitigate such differences *e.g.* design and optimize mobile application based on recognition of the client/device. Mobile application performance can vary widely based on the application design, content as well as how the content adapts to the device.

Expectations of accessible and quality mobile applications are increased continually as mobile technologies become more integrated into the lives of mobile users. Designing and optimizing mobile applications for a mobile experience from efficient design for loading *via* a variable mobile network to responsive design for different mobile devices is rapidly becoming an essential part of the mobile application overall development process. The responsive design of mobile applications focuses on reducing loading time to make it faster for users to interact and share mobile content. Mobile application content that is accessed through mobile networks normally loads slower than applications accessed through traditional networks because of the current limitations of mobile connectivity and bandwidth. Therefore, it is essential to keep developed application content and structure as efficient as possible.

When a user clicks on any web browser button s/he expects and understands that the web browser is calling the server or the internet, so the user is prepared to wait until their response. However, when users tap a mobile application button, they expect it to respond immediately and in case of a delay of a second or two, the user is tempted to press the button once again or might restart or kill the application after four or five seconds. Consequently, mobile application developers should consider and focus on user experience to develop their applications. The developers should consider all complex computations, networks, calls to be performed in a background thread as well as display a busy indicator to inform the user that the application is running and performing some tasks. Furthermore, the application should try to load just enough data to enable mobile users to work while loading the rest of the data in the background (Gipple, 2015).

6. AVAILABILITY

Every mobile application consumes storage, processing, memory, and network capacity in a different way. Nowadays wireless network connections are notoriously unreliable. Mobile applications' unavailability destroys the essential value of mobile learning, banking, health, and commerce when we consider the promise of the idea of accessing information anywhere and anytime. These different mobile applications require smart mobile clients that can handle applications processing locally and continue to run and perform the required tasks even when the network is temporarily unavailable. The availability of the mobile application is the extent to which an application is functional, usable, and operational to fulfill the requirements of individual businesses or users. This is used to determine operational statistics of the applications and analyze their overall performance concerning their ability to perform when needed (techopedia, 2016).

Normally, the mobile application's availability is measured using an application's particular key performance indicators (KPIs). This might include the overall or timed application uptime and downtime, errors, application responsiveness, the number of transactions completed, and other availability-related metrics. Mobile application recoverability, reliability, scalability, and fault tolerance may also be considered when the availability of the application is measured (Yuan, 2003).

7. THROUGHPUT

Mobile application throughput measures the number of transactions per second that an application can perform as the number of transactions produced over time in a test process. An application throughput also indicates how many items of information can be processed in a specified amount of time. The throughput measurement relates to the system's/application's productivity, the speed at which that particular workload can be finished, and the response time, the time consumed between a single request of an interactive user and the response receipt (Colantonio, 2013).

Generally, throughput has been used as an indicator of large commercial computers' effectiveness, which is used to run several programs concurrently. It has been used to measure the number of batch jobs completed per day. A benchmark has also been used to measure an application's throughput. In the transmission of data, network throughput is the data volume that successfully moves from one location to another in a specified period, and it is usually measured in Bps (bits per second), in Mbps (Megabits per second), or Gbps (gigabits per second) (TechTarget, 2015).

For every mobile application, there are many different requests performed by different users. It is essential to ensure that the application meets the required capacity before it reaches the production or live stage. Thus, the application's performance testing is the solution to ensure the same. However, an application throughput depends on different influencing factors including:

- An application host specifications
- An application processing overhead
- The types of transactions being processed
- The degree of parallelism in both application hardware and software.

Considering these influencing factors as well as transaction mixes, bandwidth simulations, user profiles, dynamic data, accurate number of users, think times, behaviors … *etc*, put the phase for creating a realistic throughput process. It should be reviewed to make sure the designed test does represent the expected production. Once realistic tests are designed, the application can be executed and properly evaluated whether it achieves the specified throughput goals or not (Clinard, 2012), (Colantonio, 2019).

8. ENDURANCE

Responsiveness in mobile application design takes care of the application interface and layout, but performance testing considers the handling of expected and unexpected issues without any failure.

A small delay in load time might be considered as a minor issue in application performance, but in real application performance, a minor change in latency *e.g.* from (broadband) 2ms to (3G network) 400ms might cause an application page load time changed from 1 second to 30 seconds.

All mobile platforms whether it is Android, iOS, or Windows, enforce a maximum startup time. For iOS, the maximum load time is about 15 seconds, and if the application is not running by then the operating system will terminate the execution and kill it. Slower hardware, network connections, and other differences in the execution environment can cause an application to start too slowly through the review process. Therefore, the developer should not rely on the iOS simulator alone and test an application on actual hardware. The developer should always keep in mind that the application's load time is the first chance to impress the target mobile users (Lynch, 2013).

In the worst case, if a mobile application fails, it is possible that a huge number of users will never use this application again and some of them will just shift to a competitor's application. Moreover, they will inform others about their negative experience with this application. Developers can create a load test process as it simulates different conditions of a client and mobile network such as 3G, 4G, 5G, DSL, and Edge as well as Android phones, iPhone, iPad, Blackberry, and tablets... *etc.* Whether a user has an Android tablet running in the mobile application or iPhone navigator, a mobile web browser, or a Blackberry phone accessing a standard website, the developers should generate the same type of traffic for the servers to handle as real users would. It is also important to ensure that the response time is acceptable by the user as well as is within the boundaries of Service Level Agreements (SIGOS, 2015), (KMS-Technology, 2017), (Humika, 2019).

9. FEEDBACK

Software quality and user experience are the key influencing factors on the success of developed mobile applications in the market. So it is essential to get valid feedback from potential users during the process of mobile application development.

Usability in a mobile application will be improved when users recognize how to operate the 'user interface' as it can guide users through the workflow. One of the key elements to improve the usability of a mobile application is to provide feedback by telling users what is going on in the application, showing users the current state, and informing them how their commands are interpreted (Schueller and Woerndl, 2008). The need to get potential users' feedback arises from the requirement, rather than carrying out expert evaluations to design successful applications. Yet, generating users' feedback to evaluate the usability and experience of the mobile application is still highly time-consuming and costly (McDonald *et al.*, 2006). The main issue in the future of mobile application development is the acquisition of feedback by market tests and finding those features that are interesting to mobile application users.

Mobile application developers should always collect users' feedback to support the improvement of the applications and to enable the continuous evolution of overall mobile systems. The feedback is also required to provide applications that fit best with the needs of the users. Enabling the users to document individual feedback about an application's performance is very important as this information can be processed, evaluated, and used as new requirements by mobile application developers (Seyff *et al.*, 2014).

Generally, the user feedback needs to be clear, simple, understandable, corporate, and user-friendly.

10. SCALABILITY

The scalability of a mobile application is the adjustment of an application's capacity to meet the demand. A scalable mobile application is an application that functions well for a user or million users, and gracefully handles peaks and dips in traffic automatically. It only consumes the necessary resources to meet the demand. Mobile application scalability is about the capability of software application, network, or process to accommodate the possibility to be enlarged to handle the increased amount of work. Scalability is also about the ability of a mobile application to continue working well when it is changed in terms of volume or size to meet a user requirement (Rahimi *et al.*, 2012).

As more and more mobile applications are developed specifically for learning, health, banking, lifestyle entertainment, travel … *etc.* the demand for an application's scalability also increases. To determine if a mobile application can be scaled, it is necessary to look at factors influencing the performance of the application such as load time, performance tuning, response time, and meantime to failure.

Creating a scalable mobile application is a critical part of any application architecture. A well-designed mobile application should have the ability to scale seamlessly as demand increases or decreases.

The ability to overcome performance issues by improving or adding new resources is referred to as scalability. No matter what type of hardware is used at a certain point, it will cause a decrease in performance. Scaling mobile applications by adding the required resources is the best case, although, it might become very expensive at a certain point. The developers should consider improving hardware, scaling out, or changing architecture.

Normally scalability issue of the mobile application is not related to hardware. If it is observed that resources are not overloaded, it is related to synchronization. In this case, it is usually not related to performance but is related to serialized access to shared data. Mobile application developers should consider scalability when an application is needed to be deployed to more than one mobile device platforms such as iOS, Android, and Windows phones. When an application is prepared for new mobile devices in the market after initial deployment. Overall performance needs to be improved rather than improving only application scalability to achieve higher throughput (Dynatrace, 2015).

SUMMARY

This chapter has focused on performance as one of the main mobile application qualitative characteristics. This chapter is divided into eight sections. While section 6.3 has discussed the limitations of mobile applications in different circumstances, section 6.4 has explored an appropriate use of memory and storage. Section 6.5 has discussed the speed of performing any task or action and section 6.6 has discussed the availability of the application when required. Section 6.7 has mainly focused on the ability of the application to process many tasks. Section 6.8 has explored how the application deals with the long-time loading and section 6.9 has focused on the appropriateness of feedback. Section 6.10 has discussed how an application can scale up, scale down, or scale-out.

REFERENCES

AppDynamics. (2015). *Mobile app performance explained.* https://www.appdynamics.com/media/uploaded-files/mobileapp.pdf

Clabby, J. (2015). High server throughput leads to better utilization, lower costs, Higher throughput means fewer servers to handle a given workload and potentially lower licensing costs as well. *Search Data Center, techtarget.*

Clinard, R. (2012). *How to test application throughput: Keep it real. Technical report.* SYS-CON Media.

Colantonio, J. (2013). Performance Testing Basics What is Throughput?, Test Guide https://testguild.com/performance-testing-what-is-throughput/

Colantonio, J. (2019). 6 Performance Testing Mistakes Newbies Make   https://testguild.com/six-performance-testing-mistakes-newbies-make-avoid-slipping/

Dobeomir, T. (2007). *Mechanics of User Identi?cation and Authentication, Fundamentals of Identity Management.* Auerbach Publication, Taylor & Francis Group NeW York.

Dynatrace, (2015). Differentiating Performance from Scalability, chapter Application Performance Concepts. Dynatrace https://www.dynatrace.com/resources/ebooks/javabook/performance-and-scalability/

Gipple, J. (2015). Understanding mobile learning and best practices. *Technical report, ICSlearnnig Group.*

Humika, M. (2019). Why Mobile Testing Is Tough? *Software Testing Help.* https://www.softwaretestinghelp.com/why-mobile-testing-is-tough/

KMS-Technology. (2017). 3 reasons why testing is increasingly integral to mobile app development success.

https://www.kms-technology.com/blog/testing/3-reasons-why-testing-is-increasingly-integral-to--obile-app-development-success.html

Lynch, B. (2013). 9 surprising reasons mobile apps get rejected from the apple app store. *Technical report.*https://Venturebeat.com

McDonald, K., Monahan, S., Cockton, G. (2006). Modified contextual design as a field evaluation method. *Proceedings of the 4th Nordic conference on Human-computer interaction,* 437-440. [http://dx.doi.org/10.1145/1182475.1182531]

MSDN, (2016). Docs, Microsoft Application Architecture Guide, 2nd Edition, Application Archetypes, Chapter 24: Designing Mobile Applications Designing Mobile Applications, chapter 24, pages 20–47. Microsoft.

Rahimi, M., Venkatasubramanian, N., Mehrotra, S., Vasilakos, A. (2012). Mapcloud: Mobile applications on an elastic and scalable 2-tier cloud architecture *IEEE Fifth International Conference on Utility and Cloud Computing (UCC),* Chicago, IL83-90. [http://dx.doi.org/10.1109/UCC.2012.25]

Rawassizadeh, R. (2009). Mobile application benchmarking based on the resource usage monitoring. *Int. J. Mobile Comput. Multimedia Commun,* *1*(4), 6475. [IJMCMC]. [http://dx.doi.org/10.4018/jmcmc.2009072805]

Schueller, N., Woerndl, W. (2008). Automated user feedback generation in the software development of mobile applications. GI/ITG KuVS Fachgespr?ch Ortsbezogene Anwendungen und Dienste *J. Roth, Eds. Sonderdruck Schriftenreihe der Georg Simon-Ohm-Hochschule N?rnberg.*

Seyff, N., Ollmann, G., Bortenschlager, M. (2014). Appecho: A user-driven, *in situ* feedback approach for mobile platforms and applications. *Proceedings of the 1st International Conference on Mobile Software Engineering and Systems,* New York, NY, USA: ACM.99-108. [http://dx.doi.org/10.1145/2593902.2593927]

SIGOS. (2015). *Why mobile testing matters.* http://axblog.sigos.com/why-mobile-testing-matters

Techopedia. Application availability https://www.techopedia.com/definition/29383/application-availability

Ulrike, S. (2014). Human-Computer Interaction. Applications and Services, volume 8512, chapter Identification of User Requirements for Mobile Applications to Support Door-to-Door Mobility in Public Transport. *Lect. Notes Comput. Sci,* 513-524.

Yuan, M. (2003). High-availability mobile applications Mobile databases and J2ME tools Technical report, Javaworld. *Wireless java.* https://www.javaworld.com/article/2073485/mobile-java-high-availability -mobil--applications.html?page=3

CHAPTER 7

Mobility: Is the Application Easy to Install, Maintain and Support?

Abstract: This chapter discusses the mobi-bility of mobile applications as one of the main qualitative characteristics. It focuses on the requirements of the application to determine the types of mobile devices to support, considering the different features of the devices such as performance of the processor in terms of speed, the capacity of memory and storage, screen resolution and screen size, and availability of suitable environment for the tool development. This chapter explores the installability of the mobile application and emphasizes how mobile applications can be upgraded. It mainly focuses on the uninstallation of mobile applications and their configuration by focusing on deployability and the most important factors to provide maintenance. Finally, the chapter ends by exploring the testability of mobile applications.

Keywords: Deployability, Memory Capacity and Storage, Mobi-Bility, Mobile Application, Performance, Qualitative Characteristics, Screen Resolution, Screen Size Install-Ability, Speed, Testability, Uninstallation.

1. INTRODUCTION

This chapter focuses on the mobi-bility of mobile applications as one of the main qualitative characteristics. This chapter has been divided into eight sections. The chapter starts with the introduction in section 7.1, followed by the pictorial representation in section 7.2. Section 7.3 discusses requirements of the application to determine the types of mobile devices to support, considering the different features of the devices such as performance of the processor in terms of speed, memory and storage capacity, screen resolution and screen size, and availability of suitable environment for the tool development. Section 7.4 explores the installability of the mobile application. Section 7.5 discusses how a mobile application can be upgraded. Section 7.6 mainly focuses on the uninstallation of a mobile application. Section 7.7 explores the configuration of a mobile application, and section 7.8 focuses on the deployability of a mobile application. Section 7.9 discusses the most important factors to provide maintenance of the mobile application. Finally, section 7.10 explores the testability of a mobile application.

Mohamed Sarrab, Hafedh Al-Shihi and Naveen Safia

2. MOBI-BILITY

Generally, the mobi-bility of a mobile application is the measure of the ability of the final application product and how easy it is to install, maintain and support, especially about its overall application mission where the application product shows the ability to perform valuable functions. Mobile application mobi-bility can be measured through application requirements, installability, upgradability, uninstallation, configuration, deployability, maintainability, and testability (see Fig. 7).

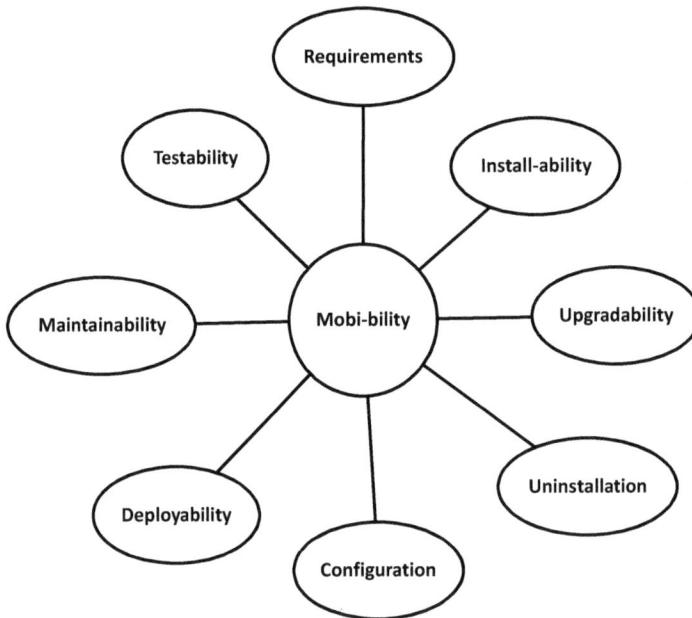

Fig. (7). Mobile Application Mobi-bility Factors.

Mobile application requirements are mainly focused on the ability to run on supported configurations, as well as handling various environments or missing components. Installability is closely related to how an application can be installed on target platforms. Upgradability is concerned with the ease of upgrading to a newer version without loss of settings and different component configurations. Uninstallation is the reversal. It focused on the removal of resources in case the user is not satisfied with installing an application. Configuration considers how easily the installation can be configured in different ways or places to support user needs. Deploy-ability is concentrated on how an application can be deployed in different types of restricted environments. Maintainability is how easy to maintain the application and support the users. Testability is how effectively the deployed application can be tested by the users.

3. APPLICATION REQUIREMENTS

Determining the different types of mobile devices to support considers the device features such as performance of the processor in terms of speed, memory and storage capacity, screen resolution and screen size, and availability of development tool environment. In addition to these factors, user constraints and general requirements of a specific hardware device might be needed, such as a camera and global positioning system (GPS). This may affect not only the type of mobile application but also the choice of a hardware device.

In designing device configuration management, it is necessary to consider handling device resets as well as how such mobile applications will be configured from a host computer or over the air. The design of a mobile application should ensure support in the restoration of configuration after a planned or unplanned device reset. The design of a mobile application should also consider the synchronization of configuration information with the host computer or over the air. If the mobile application has mobi-bility, then it can run on supported configurations, and handle various environments or missing components (Luer and Rosenblum, 2001).

Mobile application composition consists of components configuration and additional functional design and implementation which is not available in components. Two methods of configuration connection and adaptation should be supported. When a decision has been made to re-use a selected component, it will have to be configured within the environment. Components have to be linked and connected to be able to cooperate. To simplify, the connector works as a link between the required services and provided services. It can be said that a connector establishes the fulfillment of the requirements. However, connectors are more complex and it is useful to have the connectors encapsulate functions that logically belong within a shared infrastructure (Shaw and Garlan, 1996), (Dashofy *et al.*, 1999). Adaptation of component configuration increases the value of the components (Bosch, 1998). The more adaptable and flexible the component is, the more frequently it will be reused. In the design process of mobile applications its necessary to meet any of the required qualitative attributes and it should consider the possible impact on other requirements.

4. INSTALL-ABILITY

A mobile platform is the operating system for mobile devices referred to as a mobile operating system (mobile OS), including smartphones, tablets, PDAs, or other mobile devices. Currently, there are different software platforms, these platforms or operating systems are often run on top of baseband or other real-time OS that handle hardware features of the phone device. Mobile operating systems include Android which is based on the Linux kernel, provided by Google Inc. Android Open Kang Project (AOKP) which is based on Android Open Source Project (AOSP). ColorOS is developed by OPPO Electronics Corp based on AOSP. CyanogenMod is co-developed by the CyanogenMod community based on AOSP. Emotion User Interface (EMUI) is provided by Huawei Technologies Co. Ltd. based on Google's AOSP. Fire OS is launched by Amazon based on Google's AOSP. Flyme OS is designed by Meizu Technology Co., Ltd., based on Google AOSP. Mi User Interface (MIUI), is provided by a Chinese electronic company Xiaomi Tech, based on Google AOSP. The Nokia X platform is provided by Nokia Corporation and maintained by Microsoft Mobile, which is based on AOSP. OxygenOS is provided by OnePlus to replace the Cyanogen operating system which is based on AOSP. iOS, developed by Apple Inc. was known as iPhone OS which is closed source and proprietary.

Windows Phone is developed by Microsoft, which is closed source and proprietary as well. Blackberry 10 is developed by Blackberry and is based on the QNX OS. Firefox OS is provided by Mozilla and it is released under the Mozilla Public License as an open-source. Sailfish OS is designed by Jolla. It adopts GPL as it is partly open source. Tizen is presented by the Linux Foundation with the support of the Tizen Association. Ubuntu Touch OS is developed by Canonical Ltd. as an open-source operating system and it uses the GPL license.

There are also some discontinued software platforms, for example, the Bada platform was developed by Samsung Electronics. The Symbian was provided by Nokia for certain smartphone models as proprietary software. Windows Mobile was developed by Microsoft and it was replaced by Windows Phone. It was provided as a closed source. Palm OS/Garnet OS was provided by Access Co. as a closed source and proprietary, webOS was provided by Palm, with some components as open source but it was developed as the proprietary mobile OS running on the Linux kernel. Maemo is designed by Nokia as an open-source mobile operating system. MeeGo was developed by Linux Foundation as an open-source mobile operating system as well (Sarrab, 2015).

Creating a mobile application is always concerned with suitability and fitting for intuitive purposes as well as a great interface that encourages users to use. Equally important is that the created application needs to be installable on intended platforms with fast performance as well as quick response and support many concurrent users. Mobile applications should not lack these nonfunctional requirements, which users might be frustrated as they expect near-real-time application responses. The application might be functionally perfect, but in case it is associated with slow performance, then it is likely that no users will be interested to use it (Brannan, 2015).

5. UPGRADABILITY

Mobile applications are different from normal desktop applications. So finding when and how a mobile application should be upgraded is a crucial part of the development process. In the software world in general and mobile applications in particular, the application software version is very important for assigning a unique number to a specific piece of software. For example, the current version of Facebook for iPhone is assigned a unique number 2.4.6. The first 2 specify that this is the third major release of Facebook for iPhone. The second 4 is used to indicate the third minor revision of that application and the 6 indicates that this is the sixth revision, updates, or bug fix, to that minor release of the application.

The updated versions or bug fixes do not change the application feature or structure set; instead, the provided updates ensure that the newer updated version of the application is working as designed. There will be issues such as bugs and problems in the updated version of the application, no matter how solid or strong the application testing process is. The updated versions of the application always try to keep the same design and structure while making sure that the newer version does not crash and performs functions more optimally. Moreover, it should be easy to upgrade to a newer version without any loss of configuration of application settings (Christina, 2011).

An updated version of the application of Google goes through Android's market policy which enables the developers to upload newer and updated versions whenever they want. However, in Apple, Microsoft, and Amazon, the updated versions have to be verified through the same process as though the application has been submitted for the first time to the store or repository. Moreover, the Apple store policy allows application developers to fast-track crucial and significant issues, bugs, or securely fix them without any delay as in a regular application update.

As a consequence, every time a version number of an application changes, the user-configuration settings do not get lost, although every application release does not start from scratch as far as user settings go. Personalized settings of the user have a patch every time he modifies an application and an updated version number is installed (Sarrab *et al.*, 2015).

6. UNINSTALLATION

Some of the most common sources of mobile application interoperability issues are installing and uninstalling concerns. Users should ensure successful installation and uninstallation experiences of the mobile application. Generally, mobile application users download and install different versions of applications regularly. Sometimes they are kept while other times they are removed. To remove mobile applications from iOS, Android, or Windows mobile platforms, we uninstall them using different mechanisms. However, the default uninstalled mechanism provided by the application's program does not remove the application completely. It leaves some entries on the platform. For example, some used files are left in various folders. These leftover entries might slow down the mobile system and there is no need to keep them in the system (Upbin, 2013).

Some mobile applications that come as pre-installed on the Android platform are known as system applications such as Google Talk and Google Maps and examples of iOS platforms are Facetime and Find iPhone. These provided applications cannot be uninstalled because they are part of the version of Android and iOS operating systems running on the mobile device. iOS applications are essentially folders with all resource contents that are required to run an application. For instance, when a mobile user wishes to delete an application, it's generally as easy as removing an app file in the folder of applications although, the situation is not always like this, because many mobile applications install application resources throughout the file system (Harrison, 2013).

As a consequence, it is highly recommended for mobile users to use special mobile application installers to install or uninstall any applications. The installer is an operating system component that manages the installation and uninstallation services including application configuration settings.

7. CONFIGURATION

Mobile application configuration refers to the way a mobile application or mobile system is set up, the components that make up the application, or the system that works. Many products require that mobile devices have a certain minimum configuration. For example, the installed mobile application might require a minimum amount of main memory, a particular microprocessor, performance speed, video adapter, and graphics display monitor. When a new mobile application is installed, sometimes there is a need to be configured in a specific way.

Generally, a configuration of the mobile world is the arrangement of a mobile system or application or the process of arranging the components that make up a whole mobile system or application work as required. Currently, the design and development platform offers a working environment that allows mobile developers to build their applications by fully configurable settings.

Mobile applications should be developed with unique user interactions that mobile users require. Comprehensive software configuration capabilities that complement creative content design services are required to create great mobile applications. An android operating system can use the Android application descriptor element to add information to the manifest Android application, which is used by the Android platform as an application properties file. In the Apple world, iOS devices are placed in the application descriptor and within the <iPhone> element which can have many elements: Entitlements, a requested Display Resolution, InfoAdditions, an external SWF, and a force CPU Render Mode For Devices (Youngman, 2015).

8. DEPLOYABILITY

Mobile application deployment is the process of getting and making a mobile application ready for the market. A newly created application may work fine on the presented device, but that does not guarantee it is ready for another to use. Many mobile application program features might not be needed for the current use, but ought to be provided if the application is used for other purposes or by different users. The provided features are needed to make the mobile application more suitable, user-friendly, and supportive against piracy.

Mobile application developers should consider adding several features to make an application ready for different users to use Help documents, Trial Version, Install Wizard and Uninstall an application. One of the most important factors that need to be considered in making mobile applications more marketable is to make them easier to use. A key factor to provide usable mobile applications is the inclusion of active online help. Generally, any form of help including different types of help documents makes mobile applications much easy to use. Creating a mobile application trial version is a marketing technique rather than a deployment technique. However, it is a step that needs to be performed throughout the deployment process, since it focuses on making a mobile application ready to use. Providing a trial version of a mobile application allows users to try an application before buying it.

The trial version should be built in a restrictive method that does not give away so much that the user might decide to stay with the trial version and never buy the full version. Mobile application installation wizard serves different purposes such as making a mobile application easy to download or share with others by bundling an application and all its resources into a single install file. Moreover, it makes the mobile application easy to install by placing all used resources in the required places. However, mobile application developers should ensure that the developed application is as easy to uninstall as it was to install. In other words, all files that were copied to the mobile device can be removed and clean up any system-related changes that an application installation has made.

There is a lot of work to do for getting a mobile application ready for Google market, Apple store, or other market places than simply building a great mobile application. Deploying a mobile application makes it more complete, much easier to use, helps to reduce program piracy, and gives an application a professional feeling (Godtland, 2011).

9. MAINTAINABILITY

The flexibility of mobile a application is related to the ability to add, modify or remove functions or features without damaging the current application. Similarly, maintainability focuses on the modifications related to minor function changes and error or fault corrections. Thus for a mobile application's maintainability, it is very significant to understand how software application evolution works. Generally, the theory of software application evolution indicates that even if the implementation is correct and completely considers the whole requirements, the application has to be updated frequently for it to be consistently satisfactory.

Traditionally maintenance starts with implementing and testing/evaluating the software and continues as long as the application is used and available Margaret (2007). This means that application maintenance is a set of actions/activities to correct errors/faults in a software application after the testing/evaluation phase. However, mobile application maintenance is more than just corrections that need to be done after the application is released. Mobile application maintenance is also about adapting the application to newly defined requirements by adding/modifying or improving features and functions. Maintenance of mobile applications is closely related to factors of incremental changes, corrective changes, and application improvements.

Many mobile application maintenance issues and concerns are rather subjective which might depend on the nature of the application, target user culture, or availability of qualified/skilled developers. Maintainability also relates to how easily a change can be accommodated. This means an application maintainer can understand the application and approve the modification made does not break or interrupt the existing application functionality (Paasonen, 2011).

Testing, documentation, and using conventions are essential for maintainability. It is a very important factor that focuses on how an application is developed. As an application quality factor, maintainability cannot be made into the mobile application after the implementation phase. Therefore, it has to be considered from the beginning of its development. In the mobile world, the application code must be readable and maintainable. Otherwise, the application maintenance cost increases over time (Wong, 2015).

Maintainability is an application quality issue that consists of different factors including analyzability/readability, changeability, stability, and testability. Therefore mobile application developers need to keep mobile application code clean, documented, and avoid complicated codes when they can do simple ones (Spriestersbach and Springer, 2004).

10. TESTABILITY

Building testable applications are very important, as the quality mobile application requires quality application testing. In mobile application development, testing is about the unit test. There is a need to perform a complete test before release and a regression test after adding new or updated features. Network connectivity, rotation, and locales that affect the performance of the application should be tested. Moreover, testing the mobile application on target devices is essential to capture the user behaviors and interactions, find bugs related to performance, device usability, and provides a more realistic application representation of reality. Furthermore, testing an application on virtual devices leads to early application prototyping such as the ability to test new screen sizes quickly (Matti, 2014).

Mobile application testability is not only something related to the ability to execute an application, but it is one of the quality attributes that contribute to a successful and sustainable mobile application. Testability is similar to all other quality attributes. It becomes clear when something is missing. It is easy to miss planning and designing for testability. Therefore testability needs to come in the second phase when a new mobile application product is designed. The collaboration in the mobile application is a key aspect in reaching the testability of applications as in software application development. The testability of a mobile application might be affected by different factors such as the selection of technologies, tools, and architecture. Testability problems in mobile application development (designs and implementation phases) are defects and it is essential to consider them as early as possible.

To build a testable application, developers should always consider that practice and theory are very different. Every mobile application should be tested. But, not all mobile applications are easily testable. Due to some important factors such as code complexity, documentation, readability, *etc*. More often the easier code components of the application to test, get tested a lot more than those that are harder to test. Testing is a key task in any mobile application development lifecycle where a large amount of budget is spent on it. Thus for an effectively testable mobile application, testing should be addressed from the early stages of application building (Zilberfeld, 2012), (Kaura and Kulwant, 2018).

SUMMARY

This chapter has focused on mobile application mobi-bility as one of the main mobile application quality characteristics. This chapter has been divided into eight sections. The chapter starts with the introduction in section 7.1, followed by a pictorial representation of the different subsections in 7.2. Section 7.3 has discussed application requirements that determine the mobile device types to support and consider the device features such as processor performance (speed), memory and storage capacity, screen resolution and size, and availability of development tool environment. Section 7.4 has explored mobile application install-ability and section 7.5 has discussed how mobile application can be upgraded. Section 7.6 has focused on the uninstallation of a mobile application. Section 7.7 has explored the configuration of a mobile application and section 7.8 has focused on the deployability of a mobile application. Section 7.9 has discussed the most important factors to provide maintainability of a mobile application. Finally, section 7.10 has explored the testability of the mobile application.

REFERENCES

Bosch, J. (1998). Adapting object-oriented components. *Object- Oriented Technology. Springer,* 379-383. [http://dx.doi.org/10.1007/3-540-69687-3_77]

Brannan, M. (2015). Mobile enterprice: Mobile app performance: Why platform choice matters. *Technical report, A smarter planet.*

Christina, M. (2011). When & how you should update your mobile app. *Technical report, Mashable, Social Media.*

Dashofy, E., Medvidovic, N., Taylor, R. (1999). Using off-the-shelf middleware to implement connectors in distributed software architectures. *Proc. 1999 Internationa Conference on Software Engineering,* ACM.New York: 3-12.
[http://dx.doi.org/10.1145/302405.302407]

Godtland, A. (2015). *What is software deployment?.* http://www.godtlandsoftware.com/word-press/2011/03/26/whatis-software-deployment/

Harrison, A. (2013). *How to uninstall a software application from mac os x. Technical report.* MacWorld.

Kaura, A. (2018). Systematic literature review of mobile application development and testing effort estimation, Journal of King Saud University of Computer and Information Science.

Luer, C., Rosenblum, D. (2001). An environment for component based development. *Proceedings of the 8th European software engineering conference held jointly with 9th ACM SIGSOFT international symposium on Foundations of software engineering,* 207-217.

Matti, M. (2014). Dealing with testability issues some patterns for solutions. Technical report. *ATAC, ITEA, 2,* 10037.

Paasonen, T. (2011). *Methods for improving the maintainability of application software.*

Sarrab, M. (2015). *Mobile Learning (M-learning) Concepts, Characteristics, Methods, Components. Platforms and Frameworks.* New York, USA: Nova Science Publishers.

Sarrab, M., Al-Darmaki, A., Elbasir, M. (2015). Empirical study on mobile platforms selection, based on system, information, and service quality characteristics. International. *Journal of Wireless and Mobile Computing, 9*(3), 254-266.

Shaw, M., Garlan, D. (1996). *Software Architecture.* Upper Saddle River: Prentice-Hall.

Spriestersbach, A., Springer, T. (2004). editors. Quality attributes in mobile web application development *volume 3009Proceedings of PROFES,* Berlin: Springer-Verlag., 120-130.

Teymourzadeh, M., Javdani, T. (2017). Introducing a Particular Quality Model in Mobile Application Development: The Mobile Application Developers' Perspective. *J. Softw, 12*(5), 339-347. [http://dx.doi.org/10.17706/jsw.12.5.339-347]

Upbin, B. (2013). *Why people uninstall apps.* https://www.forbes.com/sites/ciocentral/2013/11/21/why-people-uninstall-apps/#1ca2d79f4be4

Wong, H. (2013). *Software quality factors you need to consider in developing mobile apps.* https://motherapp.com/insights/software-quality-factors-you-need- to-consider-in-devel oping-mobile-apps/

Youngman, M. (2015). *Mobile application configuration.* digitalmarketplace.service.gov.uk

Zilberfeld, G. (2012). *Design for testability the true story.* https://www.infoq.com/articles/Testability/

CHAPTER 8

Compatibility: How does Mobile Application Interacts with Environments?

Abstract: This chapter discusses mobile application compatibility as one of the main quality characteristics. This chapter explores mobile operating system compatibility and discusses how a mobile application can be compatible. It mainly focuses on the most suitable application to blend within environment configuration. It also discusses the backward and forward compatibilities and focuses on the sustainability of the application. Finally, the chapter discusses conforming standards of the application.

Keywords: Application Sustainability, Backward Compatibilities, Compatibility, Environment Configuration, Forward Compatibilities, Mobile Application, Performance, Qualitative Characteristics, Suitability.

1. INTRODUCTION

This chapter focuses on mobile application compatibility as one of the main quality characteristics. This chapter is divided into eight sections. Section 8.1 starts with the introduction, followed by the pictorial representation of the subsections of compatibility. Section 8.3 discusses mobile device compatibility, while section 8.4 explores mobile operating system compatibility. Section 8.5 discusses how a mobile application can be compatible. Section 8.6 mainly focuses on the most suitable application to blend within environment configuration. Sections 8.7 and 8.8 discuss the backward and forward compatibilities, and 8.9 focuses on the sustainability of the application. Finally, section 8.10 discusses conforming standards of the application.

2. COMPATIBILITY

Mobile application compatibility refers to the ability of a mobile application to run on more than one device, including laptops, tablets, and smartphones. Windows is the only environment that supports tablet/desktop compatibility; however, cross-platform compatibility is only supported by Blackberry.

To provide a compatible mobile application, it is very important to have a consistent application with a hardware environment that enables a steady experience for consumers as well as manufacturers to differentiate and reduce the cost and overheads associated with compatibility. Mobile allocation compatibility can be measured through device compatibility, operating system compatibility, application compatibility, configuration compatibility, backward compatibility, forward compatibility, sustainability, and standards conformance, as illustrated in Fig. (**8**). Device compatibility is about how an application is used with applicable configurations of hardware components. Operating system compatibility is focused on how an application can run on intended operating system versions. Application compatibility is about how an application and its data work together and also with other applications.

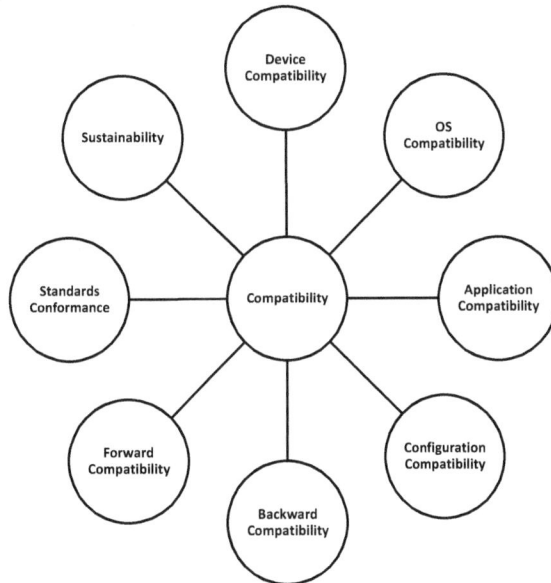

Fig. (8). Mobile Application Compatibility Influencing Factors.

Configuration of compatibility is the ability of the application to blend within the used environment configurations. Backward compatibility is about comparing the application with its last version to check the application can do everything as the previous version. Forward Compatibility is about the application's ability to use interfaces of future versions. Sustainability affects the environment by power-saving modes, energy efficiency, and telecommuting. Conforming to standards is the application conforms to the applicable laws, ethics, regulations, or standards.

3. DEVICE COMPATIBILITY

A mobile application developer should focus on what can be expected from a compatible device in terms of application and device capabilities. The tablet and smartphone are a mix of partial and complete control of the vendor. In case the vendor provides both the operating system and the hardware as well, then there is greater control over the product results. However, if there is not hardware control, there will be many different features for the devices using the same operating system. Consistency is very important because inconsistency can be confusing, and competition among mobile vendors using the same operating system might lead to clever innovations very quickly. BlackBerry and Apple have the greatest control over their devices such as tablets and smartphones whereas both companies produce their hardware and operating systems. Google produces an Android operating system, and several tablets and phone providers create the hardware.

The Android operating system runs on many different devices, with the ability for every hardware vendor to include their application assortment and make their user interface changes. BlackBerry devices can also run Android applications, along with their applications. Google Android phone applications run on Android tablets whereas Apple iPhone applications run on iPad tablets. Using different approaches, Android tablets and Apple iPads can scale their used applications to fill the screen whereas mobile application developers only need to create one version of their application, and the user only needs to purchase one app. Moreover, the Windows Phone operating system is developed by Microsoft, while Nokia and others build smartphone hardware. Microsoft also produces Windows RT and Windows 8 operating systems for tablets of different hardware vendors. Microsoft also creates its hardware in the form of a Windows tablet in this case it completely controls the final product.

Windows 8 OS is the most significant tablet device compatibility for more than two decades. All the current Windows applications can also run on Windows 8 touchscreen tablets instead of laptops. All other mobile devices run only their native programs based on their platforms. For example, iOS applications run only on Apple devices; Windows Phone applications run only on Windows Phone, and Android applications run on Android devices. Providing a consistent mobile application with a hardware environment is very important, developers cannot develop different versions for different devices (Hyung and Young, 2011).

4. OPERATING SYSTEM COMPATIBILITY

A mobile operating system is referred to as a mobile OS. It is designed to run on different mobile devices including smartphones, tablet computers, PDAs, and other handheld devices. The mobile OS is responsible for determining the features and functions available on a used mobile device, such as keyboards, email, WAP, text messaging, synchronization with applications, and much more. The mobile OS will also control the used third-party mobile applications on the mobile device. When you purchase a mobile device, the manufacturer will have chosen the operating system for that specific device. The mobile device manufacturers always choose OS for their product whereas the customer always needs to learn about OS type and version before buying a device to ensure compatibility and support for the mobile applications that are needed to be sued.

The most popular OS includes Android OS by Google as an open and free software stack that consists of OS, middleware, and applications for use on mobile devices. Bada is provided by Samsung as a proprietary mobile OS. This mobile OS has been used for the first time by the Samsung Wave smartphone. Bada has been designed to provide many mobile features including 3D graphics and multipoint-touch. BlackBerry OS is designed by Research in Motion as a proprietary mobile OS to be used on BlackBerry handheld devices. Apple has developed iPhone OS to be used on its iPhone devices which is supported on different Apple devices including the iPhone, iPad, and iPod Touch. MeeGo OS is an open-source OS as a result of merging two products built on open source technologies Moblin (Intel) and Maemo (Nokia).

The Palm OS is developed as PDA OS which is proprietary mobile OS. Symbian is a mobile OS that targets mobile phones that offer a high level of integration with communication and personal information management (PIM) functionality. WebOS is a proprietary mobile OS that runs on the Linux kernel. WebOS has been designed by Palm as a successor to its Palm mobile OS. Microsoft has provided its mobile OS called Windows Mobile, which is used in mobile devices with or without touchscreens (Lashkari and Moradhaseli, 2011).

Generally, most of the manufacturers of mobile devices control the type and version of the mobile operating system which powers their devices. However, there are some hardware issues between mobile devices. Some devices have fast processors and big screens while other devices have slow CPUs, and tiny displays and some others fall in between these two extremes. These kinds of differences between mobile devices lead to many issues and pose problems to mobile application developers. A mobile application developer needs to ensure operating system compatibility on several different devices in dissimilar hardware by running different versions of operating systems. Sometimes the application simply would not run on some operating systems or if it does certain features would not function as expected. In some other cases, the application appears to run normally for a few minutes, but after a while, it suddenly crashes, terminates, or stops working. Compatibility is one of the main criteria for quality. Therefore mobile application developers need to consider the compatibility with the major operating systems for the present mobile devices (Begun, 2011).

5. APPLICATION COMPATIBILITY

The target platforms and devices are the most important factors that need to be considered in building mobile applications. A mobile application can be developed in different formats: native, web, or hybrid. Due to differences in their past technology, each approach has its advantages and disadvantages. A mobile web application is the normal web application that is formatted to target mobile devices including tablets and smartphones through a web browser of a mobile device. The idea behind a web application is to provide an application that is browser-based and is intended to be a device-independent platform with the ability to run on any web-enabled mobile device. Similar to a normal desktop web application mobile web application is designed with three main technologies: HTML, Javascript, and CSS. The key advantage of mobile web applications over native applications is that had cross-platform compatibility. Mobile web applications are relatively fast, cheap, and easy to build although particular customization is typically required for some mobile devices.

A mobile native application is an application that is developed for a specific mobile device and its OS. On the other hand, a mobile web application can be easily accessed through the Internet. The main advantage of a mobile native application over a web application is the ability to leverage the device with particular software and hardware. However, application compatibility is the key drawback of mobile native applications because a separate version of the native application is required for the application to run across multiple devices. Besides, the natural fragmentation of the mobile device industry has led to expensive designing, developing, maintenance, testing, and delivering a mobile application for different environments. Mobile application cross-platform frameworks can easily help to address the compatibility issue but cost and time remain a hurdle for developing functionality over multiple mobile platforms. Besides, keeping an application up to date is a big issue as more work is needed for the enterprise including native application development, testing, and distribution for several platforms rather than updating a single web application.

There is another option to build a mobile application rather than developing a single limited capable web application or customized mobile native application for several platforms, which blend web, and native application approaches as a hybrid application. Using mobile hybrid applications can significantly reduce the development cost and time as it minimizes custom coding work (Tata, 2011), (Kumar, 2013), (Kumar *et al.*, 2015), (Madhushani *et al.*, 2014).

6. CONFIGURATION COMPATIBILITY

A variety of mobile platforms, devices, connectivity options, memory sizes, processor speed, and screen resolutions pose a great dispute for application developers to ensure the multi-platform and multi-device compatibility of the application. A mobile OS offers an experience of a mobile computing device that is suitable for a mobile environment. A continuous cross computing environment workflow is offered in a multi-OS computing environment. Two or more mobile applications can run in independent OS and share mobile user interaction including user settings, user data, and/or context information of the mobile application. Information about the state of the interaction of mobile users can be shared between applications, which are used to access and modify the content of local users, and applications that connect and access a remote server or navigate other remote content such as a web browser or internet-based application.

A web-based mobile application environment is provided through cloud computing where mobile applications can be deployed, managed, and tested. Besides, offering on-demand mobile application access to diverse mobile computing devices and the cloud environment helps in testing the application remotely for data access and manipulation (Sarrab and Bourdoucen, 2015). Mobile application needs to be compatible with the environment settings and configuration considering different factors such as behavior on specific devices, network density, diversity of battery states on the devices, real-world users' interaction with the application, and multiple networks (Wi-Fi, 4G, 3G, *etc.*). Most mobile applications available today depend on network connectivity to provide the required functionality. Therefore, testing how the application blend in a genuine network environment's configuration is essential to avoid the configuration compatibility and to get the actual picture of the app in real mobile networks (Reeves *et al.*, 2012).

Determining the compatibility of the target environments is very important as regular mobile platform upgrades force mobile application developers to sustain compatibility with the latest versions. Therefore, a mobile application developer must test mobile applications for OS and device compatibility and report on the environment configuration. Smartphones and tablets may act differently. If an application is compatible with both devices, it should be tested or verified for both. Mobile application compatibility test is very important to ensure that the developed application works with various settings and under different configurations as specified in the application requirements documents. This kind of testing is essential to check whether the developed application is compatible with the environment configuration (Singh, 2015).

7. BACKWARD COMPATIBILITY

The backward compatibility of a mobile application is a good match of the application with its earlier versions or models. A new version of a mobile application is referred to as backward compatible with its older version if it can use created data and files. Mobile devices that can run the same application as the previous model of the device is referred to as a backward-compatible device. To check the backward compatibility of mobile applications, it is important to eliminate the demand to start over when the application is upgraded. Backward compatibility is also called downward compatible; however, upward compatibility is the flip side of backward compatibility. It has the same concept but from an older model's point of view. A new standard of mobile application model or product is considered to be backwardly compatible if it can access, read, or write older formats. In mobile computing backward compatibility allows newer computing technology to advance without superseding an existing component.

Backward compatibility is easily accomplished if older versions are developed to be extensible or forwardly compatible with built-in features. For example, an application program interface, plug-in, or Hooks enables adding new features. In some cases backward compatibility is referred to as software or hardware that does not consider compatibility issues with earlier versions in design, causing two versions. In such a case, these two versions are not able to share data or files easily and might have different features that cause crashes or errors during or after installation in the same device (Rouse, 2014).

Apple has made some improvements by enabling Apple devices to run older versions of an operating system for downloading backwardly compatible applications. For example, iOS 5 now allows downloading an application that supports that version of iOS even if the latest version of the application is ready for iOS 7 (Russell, 2013).

Backward compatibility is one of the common issues in Android application development. It assumes that an application has been written to read and write pictures to new folders or albums stored on external storage and the developer wants the application to be able to run on different devices of Android 1.6, SDK version 4 (Donut), and above. However, Android 2.2, SDK version 8 (Froyo) introduced a somewhat radical change in the presentation of external storage on Android devices, in this case, to ensure backward compatibility with Donut, the developer should provide two separate application implementations pre-Froyo devices (one for older), and another for devices running Froyo and above (Lockwood, 2012).

Microsoft always considers backward compatibility in most of its products. However, Windows Phone 8 and previously Windows RT flew in the face of the tradition for Microsoft. It broke the application's compatibility and its capability to run on the new platform (Bowyer, 2012).

8. FORWARD COMPATIBILITY

Forward compatibility of a mobile application describes an application that is developed in such a way that it fits with planned future versions of the same application. Forward compatibility generally implies that a dependent mobile system such as a mobile application designed for a particular OS will function satisfactorily in the future version as well as in the existing one.

Forward compatibility is sometimes called upward compatibility when it is compatible with its newer or future version. It's unlike backward compatibility, as it ensures the interoperability support or integration of newer versions of the mobile application system with the existing ones. Backward compatibility is easier to achieve than forwarding compatibility as it is about the ability to accept input from future versions of the same application. Moreover, in backward compatibility, the input format is known while in forward compatibility, an application needs to cope gracefully with all unknown future features. Such kind of compatibility is planned out in the application's design phase. Normally, to support an application's forward compatibility, the mobile device/application must also be backwardly compatible. Forward compatibility in mobile computing is that the application has to be able to run on newer and updated processors/devices/other hardware types besides supporting its successive versions. The mobile application must be compatible with other related applications that are developed after the current version. Similarly, for mobile devices, forward compatibility refers to the hardware of the device that has the ability to run newer applications and be compatible with other hardware devices.

Generally, mobile applications are platform-specific structures, which function only on supported devices. The most popular platforms are Android OS, Web OS, iPhone OS, RIM OS, and Symbian. The platform fragmentation has recently started. If the developers want to develop an application for all platforms, they should have a pool of developers to master all platforms and their available different versions. However, in the case of an application that is dependent on web service, compatibility needs to be maintained for all application versions available. Any updates in the OS should also be considered. It is necessary to ensure that applications are forward compatible. Considering that mobile users update their applications all the time, for example, Apple applications on iPhones are always having a floating number associated with the App Store Icon that indicates the number of applications that are ready or should be updated (Cory, 2010), (Delivr, 2010).

9. SUSTAINABILITY

Sustainability, in general, has been defined as meeting the objectives of the present application without compromising the functions of future application generations to meet their application needs to reduce any possibility for confusion. Sustainable development of mobile application refers to the development that meets the requirements of the current application without compromising the capability of the future generation of the mobile application to meet their requirements including social, environmental, and economic dimensions. Mobile computing applications and technology hold a unique location when it moves towards sustainable solutions for the future of our world. At the core of these different potential opportunities for change are mobile applications. In most, mobile application stores there are many applications offered for free. Thus developers keep creating applications that maintain sustainability and have functional specifications to maintain a competitive edge over their competitors. Thus, developing an application that differs from all applications available in the store is very important (Arndt, 2012), (Gardler *et al.*, 2013).

At the same time, one of the most important aspects of developing a mobile application is the pursuit of a sustainable strategy. To achieve this, users can access available updates at regular intervals. These updates should include a functional extension which are applications related to the extension of features and bug fixes. There are several approaches to attain sustainability in a mobile application. The way that a developer or a user approaches mobile application sustainability depends on many different factors including the importance of the application, the resources available and used to achieve sustainability, the application maturity, and community size. The sustainability of a mobile application is affected by technical and non-technical issues.

In mobile applications, technical issues focus on whether the application is reusable while non-technical issues focus on the application project governance and funding. Commonly, it is not effective and possible to separate technical and non-technical issues. The potential for mobile application re-use is a key factor in application sustainability. Re-use of an application can save money and time, thereby increasing the reliability of final resulting products. To maintain mobile application sustainability over a period of time, an application needs to be both adaptable and useful. The information provided by mobile application needs to be presented in a useful way that can be applied so that the user interaction with the mobile application becomes easier and leads to increased attractiveness of the product. The application content and information also have to be provided in alignment with user interests to fulfill the user behavioral goals (Yan, 2011), (Tordal, 2012).

10. STANDARDS CONFORMANCE

Professionals in the field of mobile application need to realize the sensitivity of ethical and legal values in many different societies, cultures, and countries. Due to the political complexities of the countries' relationships and the differences in culture, there are currently very few international regulations and laws relating to mobile software applications. Laws in mobile computing are formally adopted regulations and guidelines for acceptable behavior in modern mobile society, while ethics are the mobile socially acceptable behaviors.

The mobile application desired behaviors are usually formalized in documents referred to as policies. Policies must be understood and agreed upon before binding. These policies are used as guidelines to express the behaviors that are acceptable and unacceptable in mobile applications, which function as laws, complete with fines, penalties, sanctions to require, and judicial practice compliance. Because of the natural functions of these policies as laws and regulations, they must be implemented and applied with the same level of care to ensure that they are appropriate, fairly applied, and comprehensive. Studies have found that people with different nationalities have diverse perspectives on ethical practices concerning the use of mobile computing technology. Deterrence, restriction rules, laws can prevent an unethical or illegal activity from occurring. But they require significant fines or penalties, and an expectation of enforcement of penalties.

In fact, at the helm of the 21st century, privacy has become one of the hottest topics in mobile computing. Many companies, organizations, and societies are gathering, exchanging, and marketing personal information as a commodity, whereas people are relying on governments to protect their privacy. Some regulations in the world state that the organizations that process or move data are responsible for protecting the confidentiality of mobile users' information.

All mobile applications including native and web applications are normally covered by the same standards for disabled people access that applies to other non-mobile applications. An appropriate United States laws, for example, the Americans with Disabilities Act (ADA), 21st century Communications and Video Accessibility Act (CVAA), Section 508, apply in different ways.

In summary, laws, and guidelines in the mobile application should be written to satisfy several needs and be consistent with the spirit and intent of existing regulations. They should be sufficiently flexible and broad to address both anticipated and current trends in the mobile area and reflect the mobile computing industry's ethical and professional principles set out in our professional codes (AMSRS, 2014).

SUMMARY

This chapter has focused on the compatibility of a mobile application as one of the main mobile application qualitative characteristics. This chapter has divided into eight sections. Section 8.1 provided an introduction followed by a pictorial representation of the subsection in section 8.2. Section 8.3 has discussed mobile device compatibility. Section 8.4 has explored mobile operating system compatibility and section 8.5 has discussed how a mobile application can be a compatible application and section 8.6 mainly focused on the best way for a mobile application to blend within environment configuration. Sections 8.7 and 8.8 both have discussed the backward and forward compatibilities. 8.9 has focused on application sustainability. Finally, section 8.10 has explored mobile application standards of conformance. To be a compatible mobile application, it is necessary to have a consistent application with a hardware environment. This would enable users to experience consisting and the manufacturer to differentiate in being compatible.

REFERENCES

AMSRS. (2014). *Mobile research guidelines. Technical report, Global Research business Network.* AMSRS, CASRO and MRS.

Arndt, H., Dziubaczyk, B., Mokosch, M. (2012). *Impact of design on the sustainability of mobile applications.* Springer.

Begun, D. (2011). *Amazing Android Apps For Dummies. For Dummies. 1 edition.*

Bowyer, N. (2012). *Why windows phone 8 breaks the backwards compatibility tradition, applications, mobility.* Cloud Tech.

Cory, J. (2010). Forward compatible (definition - what does forward compatible mean?) *techopedia.*

Delivr Corporation. The future is the mobile web (not the mobile app). Archive of the Mobile Analytics, Simplified Blog, 2010.

Gardler, R. (2013). *Software Sustainability Maturity Model. PhD thesis, University of Oxford.*

Hyung, K., Young, B. (2011). Mobile application compatibility test system design for android fragmentation. Communications in Computer and Information Science. *Springer-Verlag Berlin Heidelberg, 257*, 314-320.

Kumar, M., Chauhan, M. (2013). Best practices in mobile application testing *White Paper, Infosys.*

Kumar, M., Kamal, K., Varyani, B., Kale, M. (2015). Analysis of Optimization Requirement of Mobile Application Testing Procedure *ICSEA 2015: The Tenth International Conference on Software Engineering Advances, IARIA-2015,* 297-300.

Lashkari, A., Moradhaseli, M. (2011). Mobile Operating Systems and Programming: Mobile Communications. *VDM Verlag Dr.*

Lockwood, A. (2012). *Designing for backwards compatibility.* Android design patterns.

Madhushani, B., Silva, P., Madushanka, W., Malalagama, M., Manawadu, D. (2014). Challenges in Mobile Application Testing: Sri Lankan Perspective, COMPUSOFT *An international journal of advanced computer technology, 3*(10), 179-185.

Reeves, B., Reeves, D., Reeves, P., Richard, S., Tyghe, C. (2012). Cross -environment application compatibility. *Dados fornecidos por IFI CLAIMS Patent Services.*

Rose, M. (2014). Rouse. Backward compatible (backward compatibility). TechTarget, https://SearchEnterpriseLinux.com

Russell, J. (2013). *Apple begins allowing users running legacy ios builds to download older versions of apps.* The next web.

Sarrab, M., Bourdoucen, H. (2015). Mobile Cloud Computing: Security Issues and Considerations. *Journal of Advances in Information Technology, 6*(4), 248-251. [JAIT]. [http://dx.doi.org/10.12720/jait.6.4.248-251]

Singh, J. (2015). *5 testing approaches for making successful mobile apps.* Axelerant.

Consultancy Services Limited. Mobile application testing. *Tata Consultancy Services Ltd (TCS).*

Tordal, H. (2012). Mobile Applications as a Medium for Communicating Sustainability Initiatives *PhD thesis, Uppsala University.*

Yan, D. (2011). *How to build the sustainable mobile app.* Clickz.

APPENDIX

MOBILE LEARNING RESEARCH PROJECT

Mobile learning is a new research area that has become an emerging technology for modern education systems, which can be used to enhance the overall users' learning experience. The research on this project focused mainly on analyzing the influencing factors of adopting and disseminating M-learning in Oman, which includes cultural, social, and educational factors. This is a detailed state-of-the-art review analysis of different Mobile learning approaches and documents several learned lessons from educationally advanced countries about Mobile learning adoption. That helps in exploiting Mobile learning efficiently, thereby optimizing their use. The project has discussed factors driving the adoption of M-learning in Omani higher education including (ease of use, usefulness, enjoyment, suitability, social and economic. The project has also analyzed mobile platforms based on system, information, and service quality characteristics. In this report, Mobile learning is studied from three different angles including:

- Dissemination.
- Development.
- Adoption.

Moreover, the project provides the different type of studies:

- An empirical analysis of mobile learning awareness and acceptance in higher education.
- An empirical study of factors driving the adoption of mobile learning in Omani education.
- An empirical study on mobile platforms selection, based on system, information, and service quality characteristics.
- System quality characteristics for selecting mobile learning applications.
- A model for mobile learning non-functional requirement elicitation.
- Mobile learning key influencing factors adoption based on analytic hierarchy process.
- Development and validation of mobile learning acceptance measure (MLAM).
- A quality model of technical aspects for mobile learning services. proposing a new requirements engineering framework for m-learning applications.
- New requirements engineering framework for m-learning applications.
- A new design approach for m-learning applications.
- New software development process for mobile learning.
- A quality model of technical aspects for mobile learning services: an empirical investigation.

The outcomes of the project are made publicly available at the SQU website and *via* other channels. They will be further disseminated and used for the improvement of the Mobile learning initiatives as well as for propagation of their use.

RESEARCH OBJECTIVES AND AIMS

The main and central research objectives that were investigated in this project are:

Addressing the influencing factors of the adoption and dissemination of M-learning initiatives in Oman

The research focused on studying the influencing factors of adopting and disseminating M-learning in Oman. These include cultural and social factors, educational factors, architecture and design of M-learning, security and privacy issues, and accessibility concerns. Besides, the project was attempted to identify the major barriers to the uptake of M-learning in Oman and propose efficient solutions to overcome such barriers.

Developing Socio-technical didactical M-learning framework for higher education in Oman

The research work provided a socio-technical didactical M-learning adoption framework. It is the first time that such work is being developed in the region and especially in Oman. The project also produced a profile of M-learning users in Oman and provided the basic characteristics of those users. The project endeavors to analyze advanced nations' experiences in M-learning and the implications of these experiences on the Omani situation. The project provided a prototype implementation guided by the results found from the literature review and the M-learning exploratory case study.

SCOPE OF THE PROJECT

Wireless mobile communication technology is widely used worldwide and it supports a wide range of services including learning. The proposal project explored the impacts of national issues on M-learning in Oman and use advanced nations' experiences benchmarks for drawing lessons for Oman. This research attempted to provide a type of socio-technical didactical framework for evaluating M-learning initiatives and fostering adoption. The scope of the study is within the context of higher education learning in Oman. The research data, especially the survey data will be collected from different higher education institutes and universities within Oman.

The study endeavors to provide a profile of M-learning users in Oman that describes the users' basic characteristics. The project discussed the major obstacles to the adoption of M-learning and proposed effective solutions to overcome them.

RESEARCH METHODOLOGY

The research methodology was composed of eight work packages. One addressed the research background; six packages are devoted to scientific research work packages. The last work package focused on writing up the project's final report.

WORK PACKAGE 1: RESEARCH BACKGROUND

The research background was started with a theoretical literature review including a primary assessment of other approaches related to the M-learning initiative in other countries. To achieve the objectives of this work package, digital resources such as the Google search engine, IEEE Xplore, SpringerLink, ACM Digital Library, and CiteSeer were used.

WORK PACKAGE 2: ADVANCED NATIONS M-LEARNING EXPERIENCES

In this background, the search process was carried out on advanced nations' M-learning experiences to identify possible lessons for and solutions to barriers facing the take-up of M-learning.

WORK PACKAGE 3: CASE STUDY

An exploratory case study on Oman was conducted to test the extent to which the barriers and solutions are drawn from the large western and eastern-centric literature apply in the Omani situation.

WORK PACKAGE 4: DATA ANALYSIS

Qualitative and quantitative methodologies were used to analyze the data gathered from interviews and surveys respectively in the previous work packages using any statistical analysis tool (SPSS).

WORK PACKAGE 5: FRAMEWORK

As mentioned earlier in the main research contribution that the research focused on providing a new socio-technical didactical M-learning adoption framework. Therefore, this work package focused on the design of the framework architecture to capture the research objectives as expressed in the project objectives. This work package also specified all components of the proposed framework.

WORK PACKAGE 6: PROTOTYPE IMPLEMENTATION

This work package described the design and implementation of the project prototype, which depends on the completion of the all above-mentioned work packages. A prototype implementation was developed to show the feasibility of the provided framework that considers a set of non-functional requirements such as performance, security, privacy, and accessibility.

WORK PACKAGE 7: EVALUATION

The evaluation phase is a systematic investigation phase of the worth or significance of the objectives. Evaluation normally involves some standards, criteria, measures of success, or objectives that describe the value of the object. Evaluation can identify criteria for success, lessons to learn, objectives to achieve, ways to improve the work, and the means to move forward. The main target of the project evaluation work package is to assess the degree to which project objectives were achieved, provide recommendations for project improvement and examine the changes that resulted from doing the project. Selecting an evaluation type provides a direction for the evaluation process and helps keep the evaluation process focused on its main purpose. The most common types of evaluation are summative, process, formative, and outcome. As our evaluation purposes focus on the results of the ultimate outcomes of the project, the suitable evaluation type is outcome evaluation; whereas, the results of the evaluation should identify both the desirable and undesirable impacts of the project. Conducting this type of evaluation, needs a good understanding of the project process, the outcomes, and the relationship between the two. Then, collections of sufficient evidence during the project are needed to demonstrate how certain outcomes are related to a specific set of project activities. To perform outcome evaluation, identifying evaluation indicators, collecting appropriate data, and interpreting the results are crucial as well as challenging. The measure of success is that both the framework models and their supporting components indeed achieve the research objectives and demonstrate it by experiments through implementation prototype.

WORK PACKAGE 8: PROJECT DOCUMENTATION

Writing up the final project report is based on the results of all work packages.

PROJECT FINDINGS

The findings of the project are:

- A state-of-the-art review analysis of M-learning approaches.
- Learned Lessons of M-Learning adoption from the educationally advanced countries.
  - Develop a partnership between public and private entities.
  - Define users' characteristics, cultural norms and build customized contents.
  - Assess M-learning infrastructure and incorporate necessary improvement.
  - Develop trust and awareness, through workshops, training, and successful experiences.
  - Develop a national-level M-learning objective, proper planning, and leadership support.
- Factors driving the adoption of mobile learning in Omani higher education.
  - Ease of use (Flexibility)
  - Usefulness
  - Enjoyment
  - Suitability
  - Social
  - Economic
- Mobile platforms selection, based on system, information, and service quality characteristics.
- A model for mobile learning non-functional requirement elicitation.
- Mobile Learning (M-learning) key influencing factors adoption based on Analytic Hierarchy Process (AHP).
  - Enjoyment
  - Flexibility
  - Suitability

- ◦ Social
- ◦ Economic
- ◦ Efficiency
- Development and validation of Mobile Learning Acceptance Measure (MLAM).
- A quality model of technical aspects for mobile learning services: an empirical investigation.
  - ◦ Availability
  - ◦ Fast Response Times
  - ◦ Flexibility
  - ◦ Scalability
  - ◦ Usability
  - ◦ Maintainability
  - ◦ Functionality
  - ◦ Reliability
  - ◦ Connectivity
  - ◦ Performance
  - ◦ User Interface
  - ◦ Security
- New requirements engineering framework for M-learning applications.
- New design approach for M-learning applications.
- New software development process for mobile learning.

LIMITATION AND IMPLICATIONS FOR FUTURE STUDIES

The rapid increase of mobile applications has outpaced traditional software applications. However, these traditional software engineering applications cannot be applied directly to mobile devices due to the following issues:

- Different mobile platforms such as iOS, Android, Windows 7, *etc*.
- Different hardware makers for platforms such as HTC, Google, Samsung, Apple, *etc*.
- Mobile device user interfaces (UI) provide a new mechanism for human-computer interaction sequences such as multi-touch interfaces, image recognition, code scanning, *etc*., that have not been previously explored in research and there are no existing established user interface guidelines.

The main future concerns and challenges of M-learning adoption are as follows:

- M-learning may make it easier to fraud. M-learning users may use dishonest methods to take or copy something valuable from another person; this may make it easier to cheat.
- Finding the best infrastructures by choosing the right infrastructure that supports the needed mobile application operations.
- Creating a universal M-learning system user interface. Means designing for diversity in end-users and contexts of use of M-learning system interface.
- Design an effective context-aware M-learning application that can sense the environment and react or adapt to the changing context while the learner's learning

process.

- The wireless network trustability. M-learning learners can employ mobile devices and wireless networks to get suitability, simplicity, and immediacy of M-learning in a proper response time and accessing appropriate learning content.
- Disclosing of the learner information *via* the network. There should be a kind of privacy policy that enforces the network not to disclose any learner's information unless their consent has been granted.
- Feeling of isolation, separation, or of being out-of-the-loop. The freedom offered by M-learning opens up opportunities for the learner to work alone and isolated from other learners.
- Cross-platform. M-learning system should be platform-independent, where, learners can connect irrespective of their used devices, or platforms, for example, Android, iOS, Windows, or Blackberry.

RECOMMENDATIONS

In an epoch where humanistic values are diminishing and our vision towards social progress is disintegrating, our need to promote responsible education and learning is more crucial than ever. The advent of mobile phones presents a great opportunity and offers a timely challenge to redefine and transform our educational paradigms. As wine fans claim, we cannot pour fresh wine in old bottles, likewise, M-learning too requires a new philosophical framework and new educational paradigms if it is to flourish. Only then will it become ubiquitous. Hence, below are some recommendations for the learning system policy-makers:

1. Leverage existing investments. Policy-makers should take stock of existing ICT investments and approaches to devise strategies that complement rather than replace the current infrastructure.
2. Localize policies. Policy-makers should consider the local contexts of the country or region when creating new policies or adapting existing ones, as strategies that work for one country may not be appropriate in another.
3. Support open technical standards. Policy-makers should encourage the use of open, standards-based platforms for M-learning applications, to increase access and streamline the development process.
4. Promote intersectional cooperation and multi-stakeholder partnerships. Policy-makers should promote cooperation between different branches of government and encourage partnerships between stakeholders from a variety of sectors and levels.
5. Establish policies at all levels. Policy-makers should create or revise M-learning policies at both the national and local levels, regardless of whether education is decentralized. National policies should provide overarching structure and guidance, while local policies direct implementation in individual districts or institutions.
6. Review and update existing policies. Policy-makers should revisit existing policies, particularly at the local level, that may be overly restrictive regarding the use of mobile technology at schools and universities. National policies may need to be clarified or revised to give better guidance to districts and institutions.
7. Ensure inclusive education. Policy-makers should ensure that M-learning policies

promote gender equality and accessibility for learners with disabilities. This effort is essential to meet the Education for All (EFA) goals of providing quality education to all learners worldwide. ICT is a powerful vehicle for enhancing learning, and mobile devices form an essential part of this vehicle.

FUTURE CONCERNS AND CHALLENGES

- Cross-platform.
- Wireless network trustability.
- M-learning may make it easier to fraud or cheat.
- Disclosing of the learner information *via* a network.
- Finding the best infrastructure that needed mobile application operations.
- Creating a universal M-learning system user interface. Designing for diversity in end-users.
- Design an effective context-aware M-learning application that can sense the environment and react or adapt to the changing context while the learner's learning process.

SUBJECT INDEX

www.ingramcontent.com/pod-product-compliance
Lightning Source LLC
Chambersburg PA
CBHW041719210326
41598CB00007B/710